C

TWELVE MONTHS
LOVE AND PAIN IN THE FAST LANE

HARRY SHOTTA

ACORN BOOKS
www.acornbooks.co.uk

This edition published in 2014 by
Acorn Books
www.acornbooks.co.uk

Acorn Books is an imprint of
Andrews UK Limited
www.andrewsuk.com

Preface

Hip Hop is the voice of the voiceless, it's the CNN or World Service of the youth, stories are spoken in tongues in intricate ways that defy scientific studies.

The concept of the MC is actually an enigma when you consider that the human brain can correlate syllables and synonyms in time, on beat with frequently changing erratic rhythmic patterns. The lyrics make sense, stories are told, souls are touched. This kind of artistic ability isn't going to be streamed, downloaded, or replicated by any kind of artificial intelligence any time soon.

A lot of rappers rap, it's nothing new, but Harry Shotta is very different to everyone else.

I have had the fortunate experience of spinning for him live on air, and it's baffling to see how he manipulates words. It's actually hard to comprehend the speed of the thought processes that takes place when he freestyles, how he effortlessly slips between rapid fire flows, veraciously tearing apart the traditional use of the English language. No mistakes allowed, constantly moving the crowd, constantly ahead of the beat, calculating, constructing rhymes that decimate any style or tempo of track placed before him.

Whether you manage to see him perform live within a Hip Hop, D&B, or studio environment just appreciate that moment. Be glad you got to witness that moment because there isn't anyone else like him. He is a living enigma, a truly unique artist, an ever evolving work in progress.

A lot of Rappers rap, but very few can stand next to him in the booth, and those very few are constantly on their toes whilst in that booth.

A lot of Rappers rap, but no one else can do what Harry Shotta does.

DJ Semtex 1xtra

Foreword

When I first sat down to write this book I didn't know if I could pull it off. The challenge of writing eighteen chapters not only giving insights into the background of my recent mixtape 'Twelve Months' but deeper glimpses into my life would be a tough task. I didn't think detailing how the tracks were made, inspiration for beats and how the studio sessions went down would be hard to detail. It was more of a case of if I really wanted to share the more emotional side of my last year with the public. It had been a hectic time, full of love and pain in the fast lane.

Sitting down and writing the first chapter was a wakeup call. If I was really going to write this book and take it seriously I had to unearth memories from times when I wasn't as stable and level headed as I am now. I had to revisit parts of my childhood that I would rather forget. I would have to go back to connect with feelings that I had let go of to give readers a real insight into my reasons for writing some of the tracks on the mixtape. I would also have to be openly honest about my current relationship and not be afraid to express all of my emotions. It wasn't going to be easy but as I wrote the first chapter which details a lot of the hardships of a certain part of my childhood, I found that it felt good to get the words down onto the page. Much in the same way I used the writing of the songs in the first place in a therapeutic sense, I found explaining how the songs came about and the background story of why I wrote them helpful to me as an individual.

Some people would ask 'why write a book?' I'm a man who's like challenges. If they say it can't be done I actively go out to prove the non-believers wrong. At first it was a good idea that turned into so much more. I found I enjoyed writing the chapters much in the same way I enjoyed writing bars. It wasn't a chore or something that was forced. I felt inspired to get all my feelings onto the pages and share them with my audience. I wanted to show the general public and the media all the thought and hard work that goes into writing a mixtape. I sometimes feel that the art of what we do as rappers isn't respected so I wanted to give people the keys to our world, invite them in the house for a while and let them kick back and take in the complexities of what we do.

Of course the content of this particular mixtape is what gives the book that emotional substance and a deeper look at me as a person. I decided to embrace this and not only tell you how tracks were made but more importantly why they were made. I haven't held back in terms of detail or kept any aspects of the good and bad parts of my hectic year a secret. It's all here, an open book for you to decipher and enjoy.

Much love to all my supporters, friends and family...

This is my Twelve Months...
Shotz

TWELVE MONTHS
LOVE AND PAIN IN THE FAST LANE

Month One

My Story (F64)

'Once bitten forever smitten this one was written before it was written'

I've always loved autobiographical raps that insight into a rapper's life, their pain, their hopes, dreams and regrets all wrapped into one incredible poetic piece. It often becomes more of a statement than a song and you feel that one bit closer to the individual. You don't get this same kind of affinity with singers especially those in the pop market. Usually talented songwriters will write very catchy hits aimed at daytime radio and pitch them to publishers and labels with the hope of whoever is selling the most at the time fronting that record. It's true that some songwriters write with a particular vocalist in mind, but whether this is because they love that artist's work or because they are selling a truckload of records at the time is debatable.

No one else but Jay Z could have written the verse on You Must Love Me when he talks about shooting his brother for stealing from him. Running straight to Jaz's house and being shocked and humbled that his brother asked to see him in the hospital the next day. No one but Eminem could have put the emotional depth into records he made about the complex relationship between himself and his on/off wife Kim and his unconditional love for his daughter Halie. And no one else but me could have written My Story...

I've had a good relationship with Jamal Edwards the mastermind and founder of SBTV for a while now. I fully respect the media force he built from nothing, his sharp business sense and have actually been inspired by how far he has come from the estate he grew up in in Acton to where he is now. I never wanted to beg to be on SBTV though; I wanted Jamal to holler at me. I remember where I was when I got the direct message on Twitter simply saying Warm Up Session? I was sitting in the Parrocks Street Dentist in Gravesend where I was just about to go and have some bloody painful treatment we all know and hate as root canal surgery. The idea of being hollered to record a warm up session with the You Tube channel I was glued to day and night made the surgery that bit sweeter. I immediately went home and pulled up a Z Dot track and wrote some of the maddest double time verbal acrobatics that I could think of at the time, practiced it over and over and shot it with Jamal a couple weeks after. If you get a good reaction on your Warm Up Session your normally asked to shoot an F64 with the channel, this is where the idea of 'My Story' was born.

I wanted my F64 to have a powerful impact so I thought about records that had resonated with me most over the years. Immediately I was thinking of autobiographical, deeply personal records so decided to give the listener that insight into my life with my F64. On a trip to Paris for a show I came up with the intro bars sitting on the Euro Star. 'Once Bitten, forever smitten, this one was written before it was written'. From there I started to think of this record as a therapy. I was going to clean out the closet so to speak on a song. I'm not great at expressing my innermost thoughts face to face in a conversation with someone, but when I have the right beat to write to I can release it all on a track. I sat in the hotel in Paris and scribbled lines out but nothing was really working, I had to find the perfect beat to let loose on.

As a fan of the Kampaign mix tape by Mic Righteous Preston Play I was exposed to Preston's music as a fan rat than an introduction from an industry insider or someone telling me his buzz is hot. I just loved the sound he provided Mic with on tracks like 'Try My Best' and the title track itself and wanted to work with this guy. The weirdest thing was how we didn't realize that we lived fifteen minutes down the road from each other. When we met up we immediately clicked and recorded two songs within a week. As I listened deeper into the beat vaults of Preston Play I realized he was the man I wanted to provide the inspiration for my story and my F64.

I can remember the moment I heard the opening eight bars of the beat that became 'My Story'. Sitting in Preston's studio on a winter afternoon, I was 'looking for the perfect beat' to coin a phrase from the old school and amazingly I found it. When your looking for perfection it usually comes when you least expect it, almost by accident. In this case I went to Preston's, told him what I wanted to do and ten minutes later he was playing me the beat. I wanted to run home then and there and pour my soul all over the music, but I chilled at his and heard some other great beats and waited till nightfall. Sitting in my front room lights dimmed laptop out, I started to think about my life, the highs and the lows and everything in between. My childhood was for the most part a normal and enjoyable one, but after my parents break up I did go through a few very painful years. My mother and father had split up and my dad had remarried quite quickly. My life seemed to be changing so much and I wasn't coping very well. The idea that my father could remarry someone so quickly didn't sit too well with me at all. To add insult to injury instead of us keeping our home in Essex and my dad's new partner and her children moving in with us I was told we had to move up to Aylesbury where they lived. I hated the idea of this. I was seven years old at the time and I was really struggling with the breakup of my family unit. I missed my mum enough when she was just down the road at my nan's house. I couldn't bare the thought

ange new place, moving away from my friends,
f course my mum. Everything was alien to me.
o make new friends and start a whole new life.
uple of years of living in Aylesbury I felt very
... alone.

This was where I was going to start my story, use the more painful years as my launch pad to lyrically show where you can go from a very negative and soul-destroying situation. So on My Story I speak of the mental abuse I was subjected to on a day-to-day basis. I can't really go into much detail here but if you are familiar with the lyrical content of the song you will understand and perhaps connect with the emotional state I was in at the time. I wasn't a happy child at all.

So for years, I went through and saw a lot of madness and experienced manipulation on a daily basis. When you're so young you don't see it and especially when it happens every day it almost becomes the norm, but for an adult to do that to a child is most certainly not the norm and shouldn't be tolerated on any level.

So on the song I talk about the times I began to realize my home life wasn't normal. I would visit my friends all the time and eventually I tried to stay out as much as I could. I made loads of good friends and I stayed closest to one called 'Hip Hop'. Even when everything was closing in on me and I felt I couldn't take anymore, I would play music and I felt good about myself. It wasn't long before I started to rap along to the words and found that I could memorize whole rap songs very quickly. Before long I was rapping in the playground, selling my toys to buy whatever Rap records I could get my hands on and I was a dedicated follower of the scene. I never sat in the front room at home; I preferred to be alone upstairs in my own little world taking in whatever the Hip Hop world had to offer at the time. Funnily enough I can remember being about nine years of age jumping up and down on my bed reciting lyrics, pretending like I was on stage. Who would have thought years on I would actually be on those big stages with crowds from the UK, to Canada to Russia screaming my bars back at me.

It was when I turned eleven that I got a little bit more confident. I had stayed at my mum's with her partner David and had had one of the best weekends celebrating my birthday with them and my sisters. When it came to Sunday and time to drive back to Aylesbury I refused to go. A police car pulled up at my mum's house, two officers came in and told my mum she would have to take me home as my father had legal custody of me. So yeah, I went home but I went home with a whole different attitude.

I wasn't as scared anymore, I was punished for my insolence with the threat of not being able to see any of my friends anymore and was made to stay in the house constantly. I answered back by going mad at school, kicking the head teacher running out and swearing at anyone who tried to stop me. I had had enough. Social Workers were called in and my father finally decided to let me live with my mum. From the moment I moved in there my whole life changed.

That's why I pretty much talk about the negatives and the heartache before the drums come in on my F64. Because although I went through the same drama's and hard situations that everyone has to deal with in life I was no longer this tiny kid with no voice, going through a very painful period. Music gave me the voice that others tried to rob me of and although I've always been a shorty it made me feel tall inside. At this point I was becoming pretty good at rapping too and when I went to my new school in Kent it was like being reborn with a whole new world ahead of me. I made friends really quickly and I was like a new person.

And this is the whole ethos behind my personal story and my F64. I wanted to show the listeners that no matter what you go through in life there is light at the end of the tunnel. This is why I start to rap about things in a broader way as the song builds to its crescendo. When I say 'who are they to judge what average is, kids in garage's writing modern day poetry, want my analysis, the weak become the strongest overcoming their paralysis' I'm using my own personal story to show that no matter what anyone tries to do to bring you down, and tower over you, you can eventually turn those weakness's into great strengths. So yeah, I use some crass language in the song aimed at an individual who tried to break my spirit, but to me that's empowering. I'm talking about someone who mentally abused me for years; I'm entitled to say 'Fuck You' back.

At the same time I don't want to seem bitter and I also explain that being that 'kid in the dark, gave me the spark to make my mark'. Even the most negative and horrible things in life can make you who are and bring out things in you that you never knew you had. I guess with me, I'm always weary of people trying to control me or use me for their own benefits. This probably comes from my childhood, but it can be pretty handy in the music business which is one of the most cutthroat sports known to man.

So as 'My Story' builds I let the listener know there have been others that have abused my friendship, tried to hold me back or in some cases take advantage of me, but 'they ain't worth one line' I'd rather tell you how I turned the rain to sunshine'.

And that is the bottom line, I don't finish my story with anything negative, I talk about the positives that have been born from the negatives. I thank the young people who I have worked with in my MC Workshops over the years for everything they have taught me and given me on a personal level. I thank Funsta for bringing me into the DNB scene, Jamal for putting me on the world stage that is SBTV and I thank my long-time manager Dave for all the years of dedication and encouragement.

It was hard to write at times, sometimes listening to the bars I am taken back to those days living in Southcourt in Aylesbury, the fights in the street, police and social workers at the house and all the arguments. But any feelings of sadness don't actually last long as it reminds me how far I've come from those days.

This was my F64, my story, everything I had hidden away and everything that I had to get out. I often have to use my music as therapy and this was the ultimate tool. With that out of my system I began to analyse the last twelve months and construct my new mixtape which was to become my most honest and personal work to date...

Month Two

Twelve Months

'In the last 12 months, been a lot going on, and it go on top, but I stayed on top of the grind, played out non-stop, never shut down shop, no I never did'

It's funny that the title track to my new mixtape was one of the last ones I wrote. I can remember having a good fifteen tracks finished so I had a meeting with my manager to play him some of the new bits. He listened intently and didn't say too much as we ran through the tracks. When it was time for some much needed feedback he felt that the track's I played were a musical representation of the last twelve months of my life. And it had been a pretty crazy twelve month's if I'm honest.

I put out my Rap mixtape 'Moonlight Hustle' in September 2012. I was thrilled to be writing and recording regularly for my own project as I hadn't actually recorded original material for quite some time. The reason behind this was throughout 2011 and the early part of 2012, I was writing a weekly rap news report for Semtex's show entitled 'The Rap Round Up'. I would take the week's news and flip it into bars over a variety of beats and Sem would spin it at midnight on his show on BBC 1xtra. Now, I am known to be someone who really pushes things to the limits and tries to elevate my own personal levels so with the Rap Round Up this is exactly what I did. I didn't make it easy for myself, it would be simple to take the hottest beat of the week and flip a thirty two bar lyric over it every seven days. What I did was spit on Drum N Bass, Grime and Rap, do double time, cover everything from politics to new technology to sport to the latest Hip Hop news culminating in the Round Up often being five to six minutes long! That's a lot of bars, probably the equivalent to three songs a week and I did it for a whole year. What it taught me was a discipline of writing regular bars and delivering something that I thought was good enough to be played on Semtex's show every week. Radio 1 daytime DJ Huw Stephens had caught the Round Up on Sem's show and wanted something similar for his own show. As he represents the mainstream side of the station I rapped on Katy Perry's California Girls instrumental and Huw loved it. So much so he played it three times on his Saturday show and throughout the week on shows he did on Radio 1. This led to a live interview with the charismatic DJ and over twenty special freestyle's I recorded being played across his programmes. All the while I continued to do the Round Up, smash DNB gigs across the country, watching my Twitter follower's rise and many people providing me with the huge accolade of the most versatile MC in the game.

I couldn't have asked for better exposure than two weekly residencies on Radio 1 and 1xtra but I was anxious to get in the studio and work on my own music. I was travelling all over the UK playing ' Fire In The Booth ' sessions from K Koke, listening to Joe Black's Realionaire mixtape and getting gassed off productions from the likes of Redskull and Show N Prove. I wanted in. So I started to hit up producers, go to a new studio called 'Urban Chain' in South London and before you knew it we had twenty tracks I was proud of.

As well as dropping a new DNB mixtape with my good friend Ruffstuff entitled 'Space Jump' I began to get asked to feature on a lot of different artists mixtapes and releases. I participated in a record celebrating 1xtra's tenth anniversary, I provided the theme tune for Adam Deacon's new movie

'Payback Season' alongside Original Sin and a lot of new opportunities began to come my way. Unique opportunities like being asked to record a 'Fire In The Booth' session with Charlie Sloth.

I wanted my 'Fire In The Booth' to be something special. I remember watching the likes of Mic Righteous, K Koke and English Frank do theirs and those sessions were part of the reason I became a big fan of those artists. Anyone who is lucky enough to be selected to do a ' Fire In The Booth ' should understand the importance of that opportunity and that it can make or break you. If you go up there and spit bars people have heard before or don't bring anything special to the table it can do you more harm than good. So I while I was on holiday in Dubai, I sat out in the blazing heat and listened to a bunch of classic beats. The one I kept going back to was Triumph by Wutang Clan. I was still at school when that song came out but I remember the impact it had. I think it was the first time all the clan had vocalled a track together since ' Protect Your Neck ' and to me the lyrics and beat were phenomenal. Especially the opening verse from Inspector Deck. The only thing was the Clan's original version had a whole array of MC's spitting different styles and complex wordplay over the track which was over five minutes long. Could I write that many bars and keep the listener interested for that long? That became the challenge. If a bar wasn't up to par, it got scrapped. When the beat switched, I switched. I wrote a five minute lyrical tirade questioning keyboard warriors, bigging up Charlie Sloth, gunning fake MC's and those who would choose to buy Twitter followers rather than garner a natural fan base. So I had my five minutes of straight spitting, I was nice. But that wasn't enough for me. I had an unreleased song called 'Never Feel Alone' that I recorded with Fatal that I thought would be perfect to adjust the mood and take the listeners into a more emotional zone. I pretty much put my heart on the line on the second verse of this which I wrote exclusively for the 'Fire In The Booth' session. My father had become very ill at this point and even talking to him on the phone was becoming quite hard for me. My mum was encouraging me to go and see him but I found it extremely difficult as his health was deteriorating to the point where it was painful for me to see him like that. So I wrote about my struggles with the issue, the guilt, the self-preservation aspect and the vulnerability that makes us human.

I have a real thing in me about not ending on a negative or sombre note so I decided to prepare some rhymes on one last beat hoping that Charlie would let me go in on a third track. I pulled up one of my favourite UK Rap tracks of all time by the Foreign Beggars called 'Hold On' and went all out to body the track with rapid fire bars, lyrical substance and verbal gymnastics.

I spent a good week indoors going over and over those three pieces for my 'Fire In The Booth.' It's one thing writing new bars, going to the studio and reading them off the I Pad or the lappy, but to have to learn nearly fifteen minutes of new material isn't the easiest task. I am a perfectionist so I didn't want any slip ups or flops on the show. It turned out that all the practice hours paid off. As I performed my first track on the show, Charlie was letting off his selected sound effects as points of praise and I could see he was feeling the performance. By the end of the session I had received some serious big ups from one of the biggest DJ's in the UK and when it was broadcast and put up on You Tube fans and fellow artists were equally forthcoming with their admiration for my ' Fire In The Booth '.

I was riding high, people were loving the session with Charlie, I had an incredible amount of live work as we came up to Christmas and I was back in the studio working on a compilation with the artists I was developing. I was planning to propose to my long-time girlfriend on Christmas day, everything was looking good for 2013. Then as I travelled up to meet DJ Phantasy to roll to a show in Torquay on the 21st December I got that call. My mum's voice didn't have the same tone to it, she sounded different, she had been crying. She came out with it; my dad had passed away five minutes ago. I was numb but I hardly said anything, I almost didn't believe it. Instead of crying or going to the nearest bar and ordering a strong drink, I jumped on a tube and headed off to meet Phantasy. When I got in the car I couldn't really think of anything else, so I told him what had happened and that I still wanted to go and perform in Torquay. Phants is a great guy and has become a close friend so I was glad to be with him on that journey that night. Some people might not understand why I wanted to do the booking so shortly after hearing the sad news but were all different and the best thing for me to do at the time was to go and get on that stage and escape for a while. When we reached the club that night the promoter and his circle of friends were really cool, they were all talking to me but I didn't really hear them. I just wanted to perform. After the set it all seemed more real. I had a Black Berry at the time and thought it only right to change my status on BBM to RIP Dad from the meaningless message I had before. I came home, eventually slept and woke the next day to my family's call's making sure I was ok and that they wanted to see me. I don't think they understood this but I opted to do the gig I was booked for that night too. There was a big party organized by Logan D and DJ Sly up at the Indigo club called the Christmas Shindig and I had quite an early set booked up there with my mate Majistrate, so I decided to head up and go ahead with the show. At this point word had spread that my dad had passed away so I put a special dedication out of respect to him on line and I must thank everyone who sent me messages or rang me regarding the situation. It may sound funny to some of you but it was comforting to read the genuine messages of support and condolences I received from people that night and I think it helped me to get up on that stage and give it my all on the show. I was glad I was on my own that night on the mic, I wasn't in the mood to catch jokes or banter with another MC. And I'm glad that the set was with a friend in the business like Maji rather than someone I don't know that well. It turns out that that set is one of my most talked about and favourite DNB performance's on line. It's funny how things turn out sometimes.

After spending some time with my family, Christmas was approaching. I had the engagement ring already but the only person who knew I was going to pop the question was my mum. On Christmas day four days after my father had passed away I asked my girlfriend to marry me, she said yes and a little bit of hope and happiness pervaded through a very different festive season. And more importantly I was engaged to be married to the only girl I've ever felt I could dedicate the rest of my life to.

So you can see why this twelve month period was a unique year for me. I lost a lot and I gained a lot. I haven't had a year like this before in my life, a roller coaster of emotions, some good, some bad but I carried on regardless and I put it all into this mix tape.

This is how I approached the writing of the title track. Yet again, I didn't want a sad production as my whole year hasn't been full of tragedy. That wouldn't be reflective of the twelve months in their entirety. So I grabbed a sick track from a new producer I had connected with called Kaze Beats and wrote about how I had overcome a lot this year and that no matter how hard it got I didn't stop moving over the bumps. I also wanted to show people I was still a competitive rapper. No matter how much madness I had been through including some personal changes, the one thing that hadn't changed was my desire to be the best MC I could be. So I used this record to separate the week from the chaff so to speak and show MC's that even though I had been through testing times my lyrical sword was still sharp. I have no problem with admitting we compete as MC's. In Drum N Bass there isn't one MC I have a personal problem with. I get on well with all my colleagues and respect them highly. But I remember a conversation I had with Evil B about us admitting to being in competition with each other and there is nothing wrong with that. It's part of MCing. That's why those battle rappers can go all out to annihilate each other in a battle and shake hands and have a beer afterwards. It's also why Kendrick Lamar can say what he said on 'Control' about his peers quite recently. It's only when an artist really doesn't like another artist that things can get nasty but if there's no personal beef there is nothing wrong with friendly competition. If we lose that competitive edge we might as well become pop rappers who simply rap for paper. I'm not one of those guys and you can hear it in the attitude, content and venom on my track 'Twelve Months'.

Month Three

What Would You Do? (Featuring Little Torment)

'If you had your chance what would you say, trying to keep the music true but you got bills to pay, would you start making records for that day time play or would you stick to your guns and do it your own way?'

Almost every musician comes to a point in their journey where they stand at a crossroads and decide which path they wish to take. On one side you have the option to dilute your music, your lyrics and your image and possibly crossover, get signed and generate a lucrative income. On the other side you can stick to your guns, continue on your original path, stay true to your roots and make music you enjoy but it may keep you out of the eyes and ears of the mainstream audience. It's a tough choice as most artists hate to dumb down or change their natural approach to their music but at the same time everyone wants the music they are passionate about to be heard by as many people as possible. Plus, whether we admit it or not we all want to make a decent living off of something we love. There are those like Jay Z who admit to 'dumbing down to double their dollars' but who still garner tremendous respect. There are those whose albums stay true to their original ethos but also include obvious attempts at radio play. Some go all out for the chart success like Pitball or

Flo Rider with no thought of skills, innovation or creativity. Then you have the real underground artists who frown on any shot at a cross over track, RNB hooks or compromise. In the States artists can blow up and sell incredible units keeping it quite true to the Hip Hop essence but they've built a million dollar industry over the years thanks to visionaries like Russell Simmons, P Diddy and Dr Dre that we lack in the UK.

As an artist making Hip Hop, DNB or Grime in the UK you are always faced with people wanting you to jump on the latest trend to sell records. When Dub Step blew up a couple of years ago everyone and their cat wanted me to jump on the sound and turn my back on my Hip Hop and DNB roots. The problem I had with that was I had built up a massive audience through my work in the DNB scene and Hip Hop freestyles and mix tapes I had released. Hip Hop had given me a voice and DNB had given me a worldwide audience and an incredible live platform. I was still extremely passionate about both genres. But I did like Dub Step, so I explored the genre. I did some shows with Hatcha and N Type and was particularly into the sounds coming out of the Circus Records camp. I listened to Mista Jam's Daily Dose of Dub Step' on 1xtra and I MC'd at some Dub Step nights. Plus, I had the title of 'the most versatile MC in the game' to hold onto, surely rapping to Dub Step would just widen my popularity? My fan base were cool with me doing the underground Dub Step stuff. It was when I signed to 360 Records and dropped a very poppy, Rock infused Dub Step track that I had a bit of a rude awakening.

Record labels can get you gassed. We had shot an epic video with the extremely talented Carly Cussen, the owner of the label was on a hype, I had built up great relationships with DJ's and producers at various radio stations many of whom were asking me for tracks to spin. I had put in a lot of work on the underground. I felt like I deserved a stab at the charts and thought this song, could be the one to crack the code. What I forgot was how I felt when I listened to Nas's second album and how sad I was about the departure from the classic

'Illmatic' sound. As a fan, you get mad when you love an artist for something and they want to 'experiment' and take their sound somewhere else. When I dropped 'Out Of Control' on You Tube a lot of my fans were mad at me. Some were still supportive saying they liked my bars on the song but weren't feeling the beat. Other's couldn't believe I would rap on Dub Step, worse still there was a live band in the vid and my core fan base just couldn't get with it. I was the man who told them it was 'all about bar's and here I was rapping with a Dub Step/ Rock band running around like a crazed mad man without my trade mark snap back on. Looking back on the whole situation taught me that the people really do have the last say. You can try and tick all the boxes for mainstream success but if the people don't gravitate towards it you're in no man's land.

So I learnt a lesson and I went back to making the music that I felt more comfortable with. I dropped a load of freestyle's on channels like SBTV, Grm Daily and Link Up TV, released two new mixtapes and my fans were satisfied.

It's a funny dilemma though. People will ask 'why haven't you blown up', and tell you 'you should be in the charts' but those same people don't buy your records. This is why a lot of artists feel the need to make watered down music to break through. I don't blame any of those artists for this; it's something I toyed with myself and something I wrote about on 'What Would You Do'.

I do have crossover records on my desk top. I've been in the studio with some big hit makers and rapped on some pretty commercial songs but do I enjoy making those records? The answer is not really. As I say on the track 'I don't really like them tracks if I'm honest, I don't feel to really write to them tracks if I'm honest, honesty the best policy, music's my only tonic, I connected when I kept it true now I'm standing symbolic'. I'm being quite honest here with my writing, I have the ability to make those kinds of radio records and who knows, one day I might naturally make one. But I can't stand contrived music, to sit down and say 'yep I'm writing a number one today' is forced and the best material never comes when it's forced. I think Devlin and Wretch have made brilliant records that I like that have naturally crossed over. I would be down for making those kinds of songs all day because as well as being catchy they still have an edge. 'What Would You Do' is an interesting song because it takes the fans to task a bit as well. As I rap on the record, 'if I dropped a tune and all my Twitter followers bought it' we wouldn't have to have discussions about watering down the music or making records for Radio 1. I have a lot of views on You Tube and lots of followers on twitter, if half of these guys actually bought the music rather than downloaded it for free then we as independent underground artists would be living more than comfortably.

Speaking of underground independent talent, I remember when I first saw Little Torment rap. I was on the road and Rap City hit me up on Twitter telling me I needed to check out one of his freestyles. The next day I took a look at him on the Rap City You Tube channel and I could see why he was being co-signed and building up a nice buzz on the roads. As a rapper it's hard to stand out these days. The first thing I noticed about Tormz was his voice. I hadn't actually heard anything like it before. Hip Hop heads will remember the Gangstarr record 'Mostly The Voice' where Guru raps about the importance of a rapper's voice and how significant it can be to standing out in a very crowded market place. When I heard Tormz spit, memories of Guru's verses came flooding back. His voice was sick and he was spitting straight from the heart. I didn't contact him straight away, I watched other videos he released and was anxious to do something with him. One night well into the AM one of my favourite producers 'Redskull' hit me up on WhatsApp to let me know he would be sending me some beats. I thought he would be sending two or three. I was overly gassed when I saw a link to a zip folder containing twelve tracks. Running through the tracks, I came across the instrumental for 'What Would You Do'. Any tiredness I felt immediately vanished as I played the beat over and over. As a rapper you know when you hear THAT beat that you fall in love with. This was one of those moments. Thinking about my experiences with radio records, the current state of the industry and my time with labels I penned my two verses and the chorus as day broke. As I listened to the beat I thought it would be interesting to get another artists perspective on the topic, even if it would be different to my own conclusion it would make the record that bit more interesting. I sent Tormz a couple of beats hoping that he would pick the beat I had chosen for 'What Would You Do'. When he responded saying how much he loved the Redskull track I was buzzing. I liked the fact he said my concept gave him something to think about and within a week I had a sick verse in my inbox from the South London rapper.

Everyone has their unique path to take in this industry. Your decision on what road you choose to take ultimately depends on your motivation for picking up the pen to write a verse or bang out drum patterns on the MPC. Throughout my time in this game my best work has been produced out of excitement, love and passion for the music, not through chasing mainstream success. On my third verse I speak on the fact that I have personally turned down deals. Not out of a misguided pig headedness or a childish notion of 'keeping it real' just because I didn't feel my vision and my best work would come through working with the companies putting the cheques on the table.

People often ask my advice on this subject and there is no right or wrong answer. Some artists are better off doing things independently. You keep your creative control over your music and your videos. You can expand into your own merchandise and create brands like 'Boy Better Know' and 'Star In The Hood'. You also get to put out music as and when you want it to be released. If you're smart you invest in a company and try to bring through other artists and build a strong team to market and distribute your music. I look at the recent chart success of unsigned UK Hip Hop duo 'Krept & Konan' as a great example of this. The guys didn't have any mainstream radio support or backing from a major record label yet they still secured a healthy top 20 position in the national UK charts for their album 'Young Kingz'. Anything is possible with the right team and of course your music has to be good!!! But it can be done.

Alternatively, other artists may find the support of a major record label is better for them. Record labels have great links with radio which traditionally is the route to getting a hit over here in the UK. They can fast track you to festival appearances and put huge marketing campaigns behind your releases that independent artists may find it hard to compete with. Also, not everyone likes that hands on day to day hustle. They are happy to be in the studio and need to stay in that creative mind state to deliver the goods. A real advantage majors used to have was their ability to manufacture huge units which yet again an independent label would struggle to compete with as the financial costs can be astronomical. With an incredible amount of digital sales through outlets such as I Tunes we have a more level playing field these days in terms of getting the music to the public and achieving chart positions.

As an artist you have a choice... ..What Would You Do?

Month Four

Fire Barz III Featuring Mic Righteous

'I'm sick of these industry collab's, I wanna do a collab to make em go mad'...

Hook's come easy to some people. My little brother out of the Kaleidoscope team 'Fatal' is one of these people. I can throw on a beat, give him ten minutes in the studio and he's in the booth recording a chorus. Other people like myself like the challenge of writing songs with no hooks. Of course most song's need a chorus line, especially if you're looking for radio rotation. But if you just want to obliterate a blistering production with a flurry of bars a certain skill is needed for this too. The record in question lives or dies by your flows and your lyrical content, you can't hide behind a catchy hook or a sultry RnB vocal. When it comes to writing these types of records it's a skill and a pressure I believe I can live up to, so when it comes to most projects I try to record a track of 'Fire Barz'.

The whole concept of 'Fire Barz' was born in a natural way which is always where the best ideas fester and grow. I had just started to get a rep and a buzz in the Drum N Bass scene but true to my nature I wanted to show my new audience that I wasn't just a rave MC and that I could construct tracks aswell. This is where the idea of my '8 Days a Week' project was born. I had recorded some really nice Hip Hop bits already, but was looking for something where I could showcase the style I was out in the rave's spitting. I wanted to bring those crazy double time DNB Esq patterns to a militant Hip Hop soundscape and bridge the gap between the two sounds and scene's on a record. The perfect producer to come up with this soundscape was Crissy Criss. The stepchild of the legendary Jungle DJ 'Kenny Ken' Crissy had grown up surrounded by Jungle/Drum N Bass but he was a great Hip Hop producer aswell, who better than to create the warfare backdrop to my 'Fire Barz' concept. The track Crissy sent over exceeded all my expectations. It was loud, noisy and in your face. The arrangement regularly switched allowing me to switch my rhythmic flow patterns. I remember listening to it for the first time thinking this is the track 'Ludacris' wished he had for his current project. Overly gassed with the track on full volume I prepared my verbal assault on the production.

Getting to the end of my first 32 bars, I thought how exciting it would be to bring in another voice and another dimension. I thought back to how I was personally inspired and exhilarated hearing Skibadee, Shabba and MC Det go back to back for the first time when I was a kid. Could I recreate this excitement on a record? There was only one way to find out. Phone my good friend Skibadee and see if he wanted in. When Skibz heard my rough verses he was on the phone within minutes and he went to work. He smashed his verse out the park and had me bouncing off the walls as I took in his word play and melodic flows all delivered at breakneck speed. The next day I was up at his house and we wrote the final back to back, 8 bar for 8 bar section. The record was a madness, a collage of extreme MCing, pushed to the limits over an absolute anthem of a beat from Crissy Criss and this is where the 'Fire Barz' trilogy began.

MC's going back to back has always been exciting to watch. I think it's the competitive edge that goes along with it that gives it that edge. With me it was those DNB MC's I used to listen to on tapes that had me on a hype but I know a lot of people were inspired by the first generation of Grime MC's who used to go to radio stations like Rinse and Deju Vu and go in for hours on sets. It's something I've always enjoyed personally so after the first 'Fire Barz' record with Skibadee I had it in my head as a trilogy that I would complete over my years in the music game.

When it came to recording the 'Twelve Months' mixtape I felt like it was the perfect time to complete the trilogy. I had released the sequel on my last tape 'Moonlight Hustle'. It featured two lyrical beasts, Mynature and Little Dee and was a firm favourite off the project. I can remember thinking that I wanted to take the series back to the essence of the two MC's going back to back with hard bars for the final part of the lyrical trinity.

I'm one of those artists who really keeps my ears to the streets and stays tuned to what's going on from the latest artists getting their first break on a warm up session on SBTV or literally stumbling along new talent in one of my MC workshops. I'm a fan of the art of MCing whatever genre or BPM so I'm fan of any artist who does it well and brings passion and something new to the table. I first heard of Mic Righteous through a workshop company I regularly run MC session's for in the Kent area called 'Pie Factory Music'. A superb DJ and a good friend 'Bad Thingz' was the first to tell me about Mic. He spoke of a unique raw talent and tipped him for greatness. I think the first time I saw Mic spit was in a People's Army cipher on You Tube. Bad Thingz was right. His talent and charisma exploded through the screen. If I was an A&R man for a major label I would have left my office in London and jumped straight on a train to Margate with my cheque book. Mic continued to shine and outshine a lot of the competition. I can remember watching his 'Fire In The Booth' feeling every word he rapped, loving the fact we had an MC like this in our scene and slyly loving that he repped the same county as me and he was doing such great things in a crowded MC scene. We first met at 1xtra where Semtex bought us together for a live MC session called 'The Fast & Furious'. Other MC's were supposed to attend that night, but in the end it was down to me, Mic Righteous and Skibadee to hold down the freestyle vibes and go all out as the beats got faster and the rhyming schemes became more rapid. The session was recorded and uploaded to 1xtra's You Tube channel where it became an instant classic picking up over 800,000 views. Every time I asked fans on Twitter, on road or on Facebook who they would like to see me collaborate on a track with the number one answer was definitively Mic Righteous. At the right time this collab had to happen and the right time was the final part of the Fire Barz trilogy.

I decided that I wanted a different producer to concoct the grand finale of 'Fire Barz' and who better than Preston Play. He had produced my favourite mix tape from 'Mic Righteous' 'Kampaign'. He has a great understanding of me and Mic as rappers, but also as people and I knew he would jump at the chance at being the centrepiece of this display of ferocious lyrical warfare. He played me some incredible beats at his studio but I continued to look for that raw energy I knew I needed for this particular record. When I heard the piercing hi hat kick in on the instrumental that became 'Fire Barz III' I instantly knew this was what I was looking for. The track has a very menacing almost confrontational sound to it. Fuck that, its fight music. It's the type of track that if you throw all your emotions and anger into it it's gonna get kids moshing out in festivals, club nights and anyway you dare to perform it. So as always the track guided me to not only come with a flurry of head spinning flows, but also deal with some issues.

Some have questioned the anger in this record, but I feel anger is a natural emotion that we have to let out as it can be even more dangerous if you supress it. This mixtape represents my inner most feelings over the last twelve months and to say I haven't been angry at things over this period would be a lie. Anger is a natural emotion, it's just learning to control it that can be the hard part. It's something I've tried to do myself as

I know I have a temper when things hit breaking point. Once again I channel my anger through music and get a lot of things off my chest on this particular song.

My first bar on the song sets the pace. 'I'm sick of these industry collabs'. The reason I said this outright is because I keep hearing the same people collaborating with each other. People either stick in there comfort zone or you can tell one guy's management think so and so is 'hot' right now and they put him on a song for credibility. I thirst for link ups I haven't seen before, innovative artists getting together to put 'cracks in the pavement' to quote Kanye West, not tick boxes for there out of touch A&R man. With that said I take a lot of people to task. Those who crave a celebrity lifestyle with no substance, people who have their discussions about the scene but conveniently leave out the underground unsigned talent and girl's from the UK who mimic the likes of Niki Minaj proudly calling themselves 'bad bitches'.

This leads me to call out people in this country who seem to follow every trend or artist that our American counterparts try to sell to us. It isn't good just because Hot 97 are playing it, it's on a big American label and a few of your favourite rappers are featuring on it for a pay check. That is not my criteria when I go onto I Tunes and purchase albums. But I just feel sometimes we get too sucked in by what the Rap machine in America are trying to sell us. We readily accept whoever they tell us is hot without really being able to relate to anything the artist says, yet we don't do the same for artists of a much higher quality in the UK. It's almost a cliché to cite 'Trinidad James' as the biggest example of this and I have nothing personal against him. At the same time I think he more than anyone represents the type of artist I'm talking about, so I used him to make my point. I don't care how much you playlist him, give him the sickest beats and try to hype him into popularity I personally would never buy his music because I don't feel it.

As my verse ends the drums are reduced to a minimum, you hear Mic announce that it's his turn and you can tell it's about to get ugly. As he barks all over the intro and he spits his first bar you know all his anger, frustrations and pain is being unleashed onto the record. I've not really heard any rapper in history do it quite like Mic Righteous. I know that's a bold statement as we've had incredibly emotional and passionate rappers in the past but listen to his verse on this record or how he went in on his first 'Fire In The Booth' and try telling me this guy isn't one of the most unique and talented rappers in the industry. Mic's verse had me overly gassed the first time I heard it, he comes with flow after flow, his voice goes from deep and menacing to literally heart wrenching rap from the gut. As the beat end's Mic continues to rap as he won't let a beat or it ending control what he has to get out. I love that energy and disregard for the rules, that's what Fire Barz is all about and it's supposed to be what Hip Hop is all about. Since when did we care about fulfilling the same clichés as pop and RnB artists? Rappers like Mic Righteous and songs like 'Fire Barz III' and in fact the whole ethos of the series is necessary in a world where everyone is so desperate to blow up or get a hit they forgot being themselves is what made them special in the first place.

I feel this is the perfect place to end the 'Fire Barz' trilogy but I will always endeavour to keep that raw essence of MCing somewhere in the music I make. I think it's an ingredient that is often lacking in the mainstream side of the scene but is an element that I am particularly passionate about and that I believe to be one of the cornerstones of keeping our music special and different from the norm. So yeah, the trilogy end's but the ideology carries on...

Month Five

Superman

'To Say I'm Superman's a madness but I'll stick by that statement, I got some tendencies there far from normally let me explain it'...

Breaking down the 'Superman' track off the mixtape is an interesting one because you can take in the record on two levels. On first listen it's a really catchy radio track with solid bars, a Zaap influenced chorus and a strong and deeply melodic West Coast production. Many DJ's have hit me up saying this is an obvious single off the mix tape and I would have to agree its definitely a catchy song. If you don't listen too deeply to the bars you could get the impression that it's another Rap record where the MC is likening himself to super hero status and that would be where the nuts and bolts of the song's concept lies. Dig deeper though and you'll find that the songs story is actually focusing on feeling different to everyone else around you and the gift and the curse of having a talent can bring.

I'm a sucker for tracks where the producer sends the beat with a readymade hook as it gives me a concept to work with and the creative process begins. When I heard the hook on 'Superman' I knew I couldn't just flip braggadocios bars about being a Hip Hop super hero with special powers on the mic.

That would be pretty corny and worse still way too obvious. And I hate obvious with a passion. I started to think about Clark Kent and the Superman character and draw parallels with my own life. When Clark Kent is a child he knows he's different but this isn't always a good thing. Sure he can lift cars and potentially save lives but his childhood was never going to be normal. I can remember when I first felt different from everyone else too. While other kids were swapping football stickers I was charging money to spit bars in the playground. While my peers spent money on action figures, I was busy selling any toys I had to buy Hip Hop records. And while the kids in the classroom spoke about who was on Top Of the Pops last night, I spoke about who Westwood had freestyling on his show on Friday.

I guess what I'm saying is I can relate to the Clark Kent character. As a child I felt different yet I felt blessed. When my aptitude for rapping began to be recognized and respected by friends, family and even teachers it transformed me from quite a shy boy with a lot of family issues going on in the background into a powerful and popular figure. I didn't run in a phone box and come out wearing a cape but when I rapped and people clapped and gave me that respect, it gave me a massive confidence boost and shaped my whole childhood and my adult life too. It was a buzz and a rush which I became addicted to and wanted more of, something I'll discuss further with you in a bit...

If Superman walked down the street in his attire he would definitely attract some looks of confusion. As a tiny eight year old white kid rocking caps, LL Cool J T-Shirts, Adidas tracksuits and trainers, I got those same looks of bewilderment from an older generation who had grown up on Rock Music. It didn't bother me though. I felt part of something special. It gave me an identity and made me feel like I was part of a movement. I would hire all the Hip Hop movies from the local video shop and watch them over and over whilst my mates played football out in the street. I watched some of these films so much the people who ran the video shop would persuade my dad to buy them as I hired them out so much. I also would stay up late at night listening to Tim Westwood on my Walkman. Hearing all the exclusives and the interviews with my favourite MC's was worth staying up into the AM and being tired the next day for. I would literally spend all my money on records and would love to see my Nan as she lived doors away from a specialist record shop called Brick House Records over in Essex. Every time I visited her she would kindly give me a fiver to go and purchase a new vinyl and I would spend hours in the shop listening through the latest releases. I was doing things and into music in a way that was alien to the other kids of my age. I think this is why I befriended older kids who had the same passion for Hip Hop as me. I related to them more. I have memories of rolling with my step brother and his mate's when I lived in Aylesbury and they were four or five years older than me. They would go out and do proper Graffiti pieces and I would be the look out! Even as young as 11, I was in the studio recording music with a sick crew in their twenties so I grew up pretty quickly and always knew how to behave around my elders.

As I say in the record 'it's like I had a calling from higher forces although it was my instinct, destiny, now it's all I know'. I grew up in a musical environment. I performed at so many school concerts and talent shows it got to the point where being on stage was second nature. I was also lucky enough to have a school radio station when I got into secondary school and me and my mates would run the Hip Hop show's which were broadcast into the school's social areas. This gave me training on being on the air and started my love affair with radio. So when I say 'it's all I know' on the song I really mean it. I had no other path in life but music which is why I say 'I could never leave, if I did where would I go?' My whole direction is and has always been based around music. I live, eat and sleep it to this very day. People are often talking to me about something non music related and I switch off and start thinking about a Big Pun verse or how I'm going to start my set later that night. I don't mean to be disrespectful or rude but I'm obsessed by music and I can't see it changing anytime soon. I think it's led me to being a bit of a workaholic and a slave to the scene so every now and again I self-analyse myself which is what I'm doing on the Superman record. Do I put too much into this? Could I relax more? I finish the first verse but assuring myself 'I'm Superman I got no fear I'm destined to blow then the chorus kicks in...

On the second verse I delve into my self-analysis mode and talk about my split persona theory. Most people who know me will tell you that I'm a pretty chilled person on a day to day basis. I don't like confrontations, I tend to shy away from arguments as I know I can be pretty vicious when pushed to the limits especially with the people I love the most. Strange logic I know but I'm sure a lot of people are the same. You don't get annoyed with the people you don't really care about. It's a minor if they disagree with you. It's the ones you love who can push your buttons and with me and they are the ones I've ended up hurting over the years. So that character trait is one I try to keep at bay. I have multiple persona's living in me though and one I can't seem to hold down is the Clark Kent like transformation into Superman MC when I hit the stage. It's literally like I have a muzzle removed and I become like a wild dog as soon as I start to spray bars in front of a crowd. When I get that rush I have been known to jump up and down at a frantic pace as the intensity and fire in the bars increases and the crowd reaches fever pitch. I don't know what I would do without having that release of energy. It's the best feeling in the world, performing in front of a hyped up crowd watching them vibe off your lyrics. I'm lucky that I perform on average two to three gigs a week so I have that constant feedback and love back from the audience which spurs me on to work harder and maintain my position. That's why I rap the line 'if I wasn't blessing these stages, I'd be in rages, lucky I'm trapped in these pages, music is my outlet strait jackets I'm snapping breaking cages'. I'm a glutton for punishment to the game and I'm always trying to raise my own personal levels when it comes to creating new and exciting flows and delivering them to an audience. If this avenue I am so blessed to have was taken away from me for some reason I would definitely have to find another avenue to channel that level of energy or it would drive me insane!

On the third verse, I talk about my split personas further and the pressures I put on myself, trying to write a definitive classic. I touched on this on my 'Fire In The Booth' on Charlie Sloth's show when I talk about not competing with other rappers but competing with my own reflection. A perfectionist's work is never done and I often feel that I can always do better. This can lead to a lot of sleepless nights and not being able to switch off and just relax which as humans is something we need to do. The bag's under my eyes and the fact I blacked out a few times when I was younger through not eating enough and taking care of myself are testament to this. But I had wake up call's which made me realise no matter how much I'm trying to raise my levels in music I have to eat, sleep and get good exercise. Turning off my phone, going to the gym and getting a good night's sleep are all things I now make a conscious effort to do but at times I still struggle with it when I have new lyrics and idea's running around in my head. I call this character the demon that lives inside of me that I only get to release him when I zone out with beats and write, hit the booth or perform live. I am learning to control the demon, as I say on the song, 'to live with this demon wasn't part of the plan but it's a part of me a part they call Superman'. I have come to accept that this alter ego is something that I have to accept and live with and use to my advantage. One clear advantage it gives me is a work rate that a lot of people comment on. Whilst other people sit down and write to further their career, generate income and obtain a lifestyle of glitz and glamour the main reason I write is a desire to push myself and take my own personal levels higher. This means my motivation is different to many and it leads me to constantly work on music rather than play GTA, smoke weed or go to bars or nightclubs. While a lot of my competition spend hours on the activities I mentioned I am dedicating that time to writing and it reflects on my output. In this twelve month period I will have released 38 tracks in the shape of two free Rap mix tapes, featured on over 15 tracks for other artists and written and released nearly two hours of fresh DNB bars on my two Space Jump Mixes with DJ Ruffstuff. Add to this, my appearances and music videos on my own channel, SBTV, Link Up TV, Grm Daily and near to 100 live shows on the Drum N Bass circuit and without bragging it becomes clear that my work rate is at quite a high level. I often say I don't fear any other MC or artist because I'm so confident in what I'm doing. I know the hours and hours I spend crafting my music then the hours and hours I spent on the business and marketing side of my music so I always feel very comfortable with my position in the game. If not for the demon inside of me and my drive to keep pushing I would probably have half the output that I have so the gift definitely outweighs the curse. I guess it can make me a hard person to be around or live with sometimes because of it. It's an addiction that I know I am clearly not going to shake or lose the hunger for anytime soon so while I have this bug I am going to go all out and use it to my advantage.

I am just mindful of the fact that I want to be a good person too. A good son, a good partner and a good friend. I would never want the demon to overtake me fully and turn me into a selfish ego maniac. It's the classic story of having the money and the success but looking in the mirror and hating the person you have become.

Life is all about balance so I strive to keep certain demons at bay as I continue to push myself without losing the person who I truly am and the good qualities that I thank my mum for installing into me from my childhood.

Month Six

The Quite Ones

'The Quite Ones are the ones to watch, always the ones that you see on the box you did a madness was the ones nobody really knew out on the block...'

Story telling in Hip Hop is a skill not many can say they've mastered. Its one thing to tell your story on a record, but to conjure up something fictional but that has the depth and descriptive writing you would find within a novel is something more of a rarity. A lot of rappers will often try to tell stories but rappers like Ghost Face have developed such a high standard of this style, painting pictures and vivid imagery through words that it often isn't worth competing with the masters. When I think of storytelling I immediately think of the Slick Rick songs I heard as a kid getting my first bite of the Hip Hop apple. Slick Rick excelled in Hip Hop storytelling. It particularly appealed to me as a kid of seven or eight as it was something I could easily latch onto and follow. You have to remember I was a small child addicted to Hip Hop so a lot of the more adult themes weren't particularly things I could relate to. When I heard Slick Rick's 'Children's Story' I was blown away. The story was simple enough but it was the way Rick told it. I used to close my eyes in my room in Aylesbury and I could picture the story line frame for frame. Although

I did later see a video for the song, it was almost as though it didn't need it as it sparked my imagination and I created my own video in my head. Slick Rick managed to take me somewhere else with that record, much in the same way Biggie would years later with 'Story To Tell' on his second album. I tried to write some story raps in my early days of writing lyrics but the descriptive wordplay could never compete with the Slick Rick, Biggie and Ghostface record's I admired so much so the bar's pretty much stayed inside the margins of my many pads.

I completely wrote 'The Quite One's by accident but as writers know the best things often happen that way. I'll always remember how this track came about too because of the bizarre circumstances that probably led to me to sitting down and composing it. I had been at the studio with Flexplicit recording the track 'Monsta'. It was the first time I had met Flex and he bought Faizer with him so it was one of those vibes sessions. We got the recording done and the atmosphere in the studio was electric. Flex and Faiz left to hit another studio session and I continued to lay some more vocals. As I was walking out of the studio towards the gates and on my way to the Off Licence I slipped on the wet floor and fell on my ankle. I felt slightly light headed and sick for a second and the pain was pretty intense so I realized that I had done a bit of damage. I don't really like causing a fuss though so after I had a drink of water and chilled for ten minutes I decided to head home. My foot was hurting but I thought it would be alright by morning time and I went to bed. When I woke up in the middle of the night in agony by how much pain I was in, I realized I was wrong. My girlfriend convinced me that this wasn't something I could shrug off so with her help I had to hop my way down the stairs as the bloody lift was out of order and get myself to the hospital.

Now I'm a man who hates dentists, doctors and particularly hospitals. If I get a cold I buy Lemsip, if I feel ill I look it up on line and although I have regular check-ups now I avoided the dentist chair for over ten years. So I'm sitting in the waiting room of this hospital at 3 AM in the morning, pissed. My foot is killing me and all I can do is wait to be seen. After a two hour wait I'm finally shuffled from room to room getting various X ray's and tests done. The final prognosis is that I'm lucky not to have broken a bone but I've got a severe sprain and I have to rest my foot for four to five days. Four to five days of staying in with my foot resting on a cushion while I drink cups of tea, grow a Rick Ross beard and watch day time tele? That sounds alright for an hour or two but four to five day's? For an active person that is the definition of hell! But what could I do, doctors' orders are just that and I didn't want to make it any worse.

It was the third night into my period of rest that I wrote 'The Quite One's. I guess I felt a bit isolated as it was literally around 2 AM in the morning and I was alone in the front room when I wrote it. I was looking through beats and came across something that Z Dot had given me about a month ago. I had gone to his studio and recorded quite a radio friendly track but before we left he played me some of his more Grimy productions and I left with the beat that became the 'The Quite Ones'. As I played the instrumental a few times, the phrase 'the quite ones are the ones to watch' kept going round in my head. At this point, I didn't think I was going to write a story rap at all. I planned to write a track about myself being quite a reserved character in general but someone who comes to life on the mic and in the studio. I wanted to put across my opinion that whilst some people make a lot of noise and shout a lot, it's often the quite ones who keep their heads down and get on with things that are the ones to watch for. The thing was as the next line flowed onto the page I realized that I was actually writing about something much deeper. The so called voiceless 'Quite One', on the estate who nobody seems to notice until it's too late. We've all heard terrible stories on the news where a loner who feels isolated and rejected from society, subsequently takes out his rage on innocent people within the community. And how many times have we heard locals on the news reflect on how that person was so quite or even a polite or reserved individual who kept themselves to themselves? All too often...

I decided to explore this type of character through the art of Hip Hop storytelling. For some reason the words began to flow like they never had before. I painted the picture of the 'quite one' who didn't say 'boo to a goose, bopped in the shop with the same top, for bare packs of Super Noodles, pack of Mayfair and an Alco Pop'. As I developed this character further, I spoke about the reasons why he feels like he's out for payback. I also hinted at the fact he may have murdered two people already and that the story would unfold and tell you why. Perhaps, he was bullied to the point where he couldn't take it anymore, maybe he was your neighbour full of self-hatred, pushed to the limits self-harming on the other side of your TV on a crash course of self harm and twisted revenge.

As I rap the line, 'he gets closer you're in certain danger' the audience ascertain a picture in their heads of a psychotic neighbour who is about to prey on his victims next door and commit heinous acts of violence. However, this was the point that I began to twist up the story line a bit. Sure, it would have been easy to tell the story of the secluded loner preying on the perfect couple next door but that would be way too obvious. What if the couple weren't so innocent themselves? Let's blur the picture a bit and see what happens when he gets closer and this particular couple are in 'certain danger'.

First of all I wanted the audience to know why the chosen couple are his point of attack. It is just the fact that they live next door to him. Surely this isn't a crime of circumstance? As I rap the following lines the motive begins to become transparent.

'Jealous of what you and your husband have, he ain't got nobody, kicked out by his dad, mum left with a next man when he was a youth, ex girl now with his

ex-best friend (SLAG), all over the photo's in a red marker, he hates any girl, his heart beats faster but when we walks past her he smiles sick thoughts in his mind are clouded with laughter'.

So it would seem his motive isn't purely circumstance and random. His reasoning at a premeditated attack on the couple next door is one of cold jealousy. From the little contact he has had with them, he sees them as a mature couple who have everything he wished he could have had with his estranged girlfriend we now know has run off with his best friend. It's bad enough she has left him, but to leave with his so called best friend add's serious insult to injury. His hatred for women really stems from a resentment of his mother leaving him as child with a father who kicked him out of the family home. The one person he appeared to trust was his partner who has now betrayed him, leaving with another man who happens to be his best friend. He is now a bitter and twisted soul surrounded by photos of his ex with slag in red marker written over the photographic memories of their times together. He is sinking deeper into a pool of depression and he is consumed with rage and anger. As he ascends into absolute isolation he sees his female neighbour as the physical embodiment of the female's he hate's for leaving him in his current predicament. Just to kill would be too simple though so he hatches an evil plan to charm the older next door neighbour, perhaps even make her fall in love with him and just when she has put her trust in this monster, he will cruelly take her life in a bitter episode of revenge.

At this point, the story was beginning to take shape so I looked at the female next door and decided to spice things up a bit more. As I thought about the plot I realized something wasn't quite sitting right with me. If they were the perfect couple living a perfect married life like our twisted centrepiece thinks, why would she cheat on her husband so willingly? Of course they couldn't be the perfect married couple. Maybe the outside world's perception of them would be that, but behind closed doors our story tells you a different tale.

'She thinks he's harmless, bored housewife sick and tired of her husband cause he gets plastered in the pub more time comes home beats her like a sick barsted'.

So this is why she is so willingly charmed by this younger neighbour who suddenly takes a shine to her. She isn't in a perfect relationship with her husband. In fact she is a victim of domestic abuse; the punching bag of an alcoholic husband who on the surface goes to work and lives on the right side of society but in private he's a bully who yet again takes his own frustrations in life out on his wife. This is the twist on the twist I was looking for when I wrote my story raps in the past. Who really is the quite one? Could the quite one actually be this abusive husband? Is he the quite one I speak of in the opening lines of the track? A polite yet quite man, who no one in the area really notices as he goes to and from a respectable job popping into the shop for supplies going home for a night in front of the TV with his wife.

Or is someone else the quite one???

As the storyline builds we are given an insight into the husband a little more. Whilst his wife is now having an affair with our psychotic centre piece next door, he is having a terrible time at work, failing to meet the demands of the company and falling short of hitting targets. He himself is now sinking into a deeper pit of depression and self-hatred. When the boss call's him into his office to give him his marching orders this is the final straw and he turns on the boss with a weapon he toyed with taking his own life with. This is someone who can no longer stand to look at his own reflection. He hates the middle aged man he has become, he hates the fact his only companion is alcohol and trapped in a vicious cycle he takes it out on his wife, action's he deeply regrets adding to his self-hate mechanism. This is someone who is pushed to his absolute limits so as he plunges his would be suicide knife into his bosses' chest he realizes he has reached the point of no return.

As the story quickly moves to him entering his home ordering his wife to 'get down here, we gotta go now quick', the story rapidly turns into a violent and rapid crescendo of murder. Running up the stairs to grab his wife so they can escape before the police arrive to arrest him for the brutal killing of his boss, he discovers his young next door neighbour in bed with his wife. Fully caught in the act the husband see's red, and taking the knife he has just slayed his boss with, he delivers multiple stab wounds to the body of the young man having sex with his wife. So the husband was the quite one? The one to watch? The one with the real tendency and ability to kill two people in the space of a day?

Maybe not...

It would have been easy to end the story here but then I thought about another possibility. Could the wife really be the one to watch? Sure, she had an affair but other than that she has remained the only real innocent party in a web of deceit, lies, revenge and pre mediated murder. She has real motive for revenge and murder. The cunning young man next door had tricked her into bed, her husband was a bully who created a regime of terror and fear in their own home and now he had stormed into the bedroom and taken the life of a man she believed she loved and was her true saviour. The irony and real truth that this so called saviour was plotting to kill her using sex and the promise of true love as a way to get closer to her. But she would never know that. So thinking of all the beatings, the years of loveless sex and staring at her lover's dead body on the floor the REAL quite one strikes back and plunges the blade deep in the chest of her husband killing him instantly in a crime of passion. As the words of the song suggest, 'two wrong's they don't make a right but in her mind he was an abusive partner who killed her saviour in reality he saved her from a psychotic neighbour'. She was now the 'Quite One' to watch and the lyrics return to the original hook but now telling the story of the lady in question stating 'she was the one nobody suspected pushed to the limits, hit back for the timid, the jail cell locks as she stares into darkness knowing her life is finished'.

The story doesn't really have a message, it's a pretty grim and shocking tale and the fact that the only real innocent party ends up in languishing in prison isn't Hollywood at all. But life isn't Hollywood. I sometimes watch films and I want the unexpected to happen, I don't always want the goodie to win and the villain to be shot up in a pool of blood. Life isn't like this, we live in a world of injustice and we often read horrible stories in the paper and see them on the news. My story is completely fictional but it feels real and authentic to me. In all my years of trying to write a story rap I had never come up with one that had the twists and the depth of 'The Quite One's. The circumstances around me writing it probably helped me shape the idea. Just a minor feeling of isolation and boredom sparked the subject matter but it becoming a tale of the unexpected is what I'm more proud of.

Month Seven

4 Lions Featuring Trigga, Dreps & P Money

'What you know about them secret haters, man who act nice to ya face, pagans won't talk direct when you buck em on road but their quick to diss you on their Facebook status'.

The whole 4 Lions record was purely inspired by the beat. I had been running up and down the motorway all year doing show's and aswell as the more conscious thought provoking Hip Hop I love to listen to a bunch of gassed up rappers talking smack. The beats are ultra-aggressive, they keep the energy up on long journeys and above all they keep me in a high energy mode that I am known for on my DnB sets. If I listen to too much mellow music on the road am I going to be carrying that hype into the club for my own set? I'm not sure, but when I tweet what I'm listening to a lot of my own followers are often confused by my choice of rappers. Because I personally keep my bars conscious and am more known for that side of spitting people have a perception that I should or only do listen to those types of artists. This couldn't be further from the truth. As much as I love Talib Kweli, Common Sense and those types of rappers I also enjoy West Coast artists like Nipsey Hustle and ultra-hype MC's like Meek Mill, Tempz and Juicy J. I think the most played mix tape for me in the past year was Fekky's 'Come on Den'. The energy on that tape is ridiculous. Fekky's an absolute beast with undeniable charisma on the mic and the in your face productions from the moment the tape starts till it finishes had me reaching for the rewind button in a frenzy. People often forget that music is entertainment and is supposed to provoke a response, whether it makes you think, makes you cry or it gets you hyped up and makes you want to jump around like a maniac in your front room. Being such a fan of the more gassed up style of Rap, I had to have at least one track like that on my mixtape. When YG Beats sent me a 20 second clip of the instrumental that became '4 Lions' on 'What's App' I knew this was that track.

First of all, the beat is a monster. It sounds like a really bad argument building up to a tense and provocative altercation which builds into a mosh pit of aggression. When it kicks in it has you on the edge of your seat, it sounds like the moment before a fight breaks out but just as you think the first punch is going to be thrown it breaks down. The beat completely filters out and creates a lovely notion of the quite before the storm. Of course when it kicks back in it symbolizes a riot breaking out, punches and kicks being thrown from every angle. This record actually has parallels with elements of Drum N Bass I first fell in love with as a teenager. It doesn't sound anything like a DNB song but it reminds me of some of my favourite Dillinja records in the way the intro would lead listeners into a false sense of security. Dillinja would often start his songs with really melodic and sometimes deep and soulful vocals. These days the drop would lead into an even more commercial aimed at the Radio 1 playlist and festival bookings. But Dillinja would go from the nicest intro's into the dirtiest filthy and earth shattering drops you could ever imagine to hear. I loved that contrast as a listener and this record bought to those feelings back to me.

When I sat down and wrote my verse on this song, I was fascinated with people's behaviour on social network sites. Some individual's Twitter or Facebook personas don't reflect who they really are. I've gone as far to say I like people in real life but I can't stand them on Twitter. A nice normal guy turns into superman on a twitter page, full of gassed up opinions with little room for discussion or debate. People throw indirects at people in their own social group then go out for a drink with the same people on a Friday night. As an artist we often see this in the form of what we call 'keyboard warriors'. The very same person who comes up to you and asks you for a photo will jump on your latest you tube video and cuss you from the safety of their home. And I'm not talking about constructive criticism and a right to an opinion here. I'm talking about cussing!! I like to call these people 'Secret haters' and I know I have plenty of them. So as my opening bars on the record say 'What you know about them secret haters, man who act nice to ya face, pagans won't talk direct when you buck em on road but their quick to diss you on their Facebook status'. It's a subject that I want to go into more detail in a track in the future as I find the way people use these sites hilarious at times. But on this song, I just wanted to let them know that I can see the sly moves and the side line hating. I know there preeing and its cool just don't play me for a fool or take my kindness for weakness. For the rest of my verse I didn't want to go in too conceptual though. I just wanted to spit a flurry of gassed up bars to get people energized but I dip in out of braggadocios lines about my own kudos in the scene, the impact of my Rap Round Series and the fact that I feel I haven't changed. I'm still here, with the same principles, the same Gold tin of Special Brew and I'm still in the hot seat with my finger on the pulse.

When thinking of the way the song filters out then breaks back into the abrasive beat, I wanted to take advantage of that and make this record a roller coaster for the listener. Much in the same way a fair ground ride goes up in the air then drops the passengers, I wanted the ride on this song to be as exciting as the drop. So rather than write a gassed up hook and keep the song as a standard radio structure with me riding the filtered intro I decided I wanted a different voice bringing something unique and exciting to that ride. Due to the power of the instrumental, I couldn't just get any MC's on this. I needed three powerhouses, three voices that stand out in the crowd. Three characters who would each bring another element to the record. I needed three lions to make this track reach the level's I imagined in my head. This is how I came up with the '4 Lion's' title and concept. Four ferocious verbal assaults coming in and out of the beat with no hooks and as lion's are seen to be the kings of the jungle I decided on that on the title and looked around for MC's I wanted to get on the record.

The first artist I decided to holler at was DNB legend and Mancunian MC Trigga. Growing up as a fan of Drum N Bass I always looked forward to sets with Trigga on them at the raves. Along with Bassman, Trigga repped for the 'Shadow Demon Coalition' and they bought a whole different approach to MCing on the DnB tempo. Whilst the likes of Shabba, Skibadee and Det spat rhymes at breakneck speed to match the speed of the drums, Trigga and Bass came with a unique half time flow. But it wasn't just that that was unique about them, it was there Northern accents that added a whole different twist to the DNB mix. When I first started spitting to Drum N Bass I was looking forward to meeting Trigga as he was someone I had always admired. He was sick on Drums but he also collaborated with artists on the Grime scene like Skepta, JME and Wiley. When we met we got on really well, he was very supportive of me on line and every time we worked together on a set the energy levels were always high and the vibes were always good. You know with some people you meet them and you take a liking to that person? Trigga is one of those people, one of the realest and respected MC's in the underground circuit who's name commands respect across the genre's and on the roads. We had been talking about jumping on a record together for a while, but due to our busy schedules it never happened. When I sent him my verse on the '4 Lions' record he hit me back, hyped and arranged some studio time with the legendary Zed Bias to record his verse. Within a week I had a treat in my mail box, the verse from Trigga for the track and he had gone in!!!

> *'It's Moss Side Trigga in the building mother fuckers better know we go hard don't play around, music in any weather we be keeping it together got goons that still wanna spray a round, bitch n***s wanna tweet when I see em in the streets or the rave I be like yo say it now, the only bad boy you know is Will Smith stop holding up ya waist cause you ain't gonna spray a round!'*

He set it off lovely and as the beat kicked in he continued to go hard, killing it with hard bars and dope punch lines further adding to his credentials in the scene and solidifying his position as a microphone champion. I remember telling him that I couldn't have asked for a better verse. Overly happy with the direction of the record I began to formulate ideas of who the third lion could potentially be. As a man who loves's contrast I didn't want the next voice on the rollercoaster ride to be similar to Trigga's in style or substance. I kicked back and played the half recorded track over and over and after about an hour it came to me, the third lion would have to a beast from my own pack of lions, the third space on the record belonged to Dreps.

Just to give you guys a bit of background on how long I have known Dreps and how tight we have become, I want to take you back to the beginning. I went to a Kool London event in Brighton and out in the smoking area there was this loud character. Tall, commanding and very knowledgeable on the state of the Drum N Bass scene but very forthright with his opinions. He had a lot to say and I agreed with everything that came out of his mouth. I thought he was just a follower of the scene at first, but took an instant liking to him. The way he broke down his points and idea's was done with force yet humour. It wasn't till Funsta and Skibadee put me up on the fact that he was a budding MC with bags of potential that I really knew he was interested in that side of things. He wasn't one of those up and coming guys, who grab you as you're walking to the stage, spit a load of bars in your ear and ask you to help them get on in the game. He wasn't begging for anything, he was just doing his own thing. From when I first heard him spit and other MC's immediately begin to remix his flows I knew he had something special. We started to link up on the regular and as I grew in the scene I decided I wanted to help other artists in the studio and develop new talent. Dreps was at the top of my list to work with. He had smashed two studio mixes in the DNB scene, bought new flows to the table and had created a growing fan base all over the UK. Above all to me though he has a unique persona and presence every time he walks into a room that a lot of artists lack. I've seen Dreps put in the hours and the hard work. He is a perfectionist in the booth and is always trying to come up with new flows and creative ways of putting his ideas across through music. We went to the studio to work on '4 Lions' and not content with having one verse prepared he showed me possible verses he had written. Both were tight, but we decided to take parts from both to create something sick, fusing the wickedest elements of each sixteen bar verse. I love the way his tone on the song starts calm as he warn's adversaries to not 'start him off like the spark of a bomb at the start of the war' then just before the drums kick in he tells his competitors 'I've seen what you're on its not seeming a lot'. As he rips into his verse he laughs at the audacity of rappers who have jumped on others flows and are getting props and kudos from ideas that aren't even their own. He peppers the verse with his trademark ad-lib's and his personality shines throughout the performance. I can't deny that I was proud playing his verse back in the studio. He provided the record with the perfect twist it needed. The third young lion roared and put it down properly in the overcrowded Jungle of MC's staking their claim for the title.

With the record at this stage I wanted the last voice on the track to be a recognisable one. I thought of all the rapper's I had had on constant rotation over the years and I tried to put myself in the shoes of the audience. Who would I want to hear at the end of a record like this? One name kept coming to mind... P Money.

I had been a fan of P from the moment I heard 'What Did He Say'. As a fan of high energy music and particularly the early days of Grime it was only natural that I would like an artist like P Money. I respected him because he bought something else to the picture. The Grime scene has given us some incredible talent and has done in lot in terms of smashing down barriers on the UK scene. P came into the scene like a tornado. He quickly rose to the top of the ranks in the Grime scene, through high profile clashes and his mix tape 'Money over Everything'. I have to shout Fatal as well because he would bring out P Money sets out when we would hit the road travelling to Drum N Bass gigs and it wasn't long before we knew his lyrics word for word. A lot of the sets also featured members of the OG'z Collective such as Blacks and Little Dee, two other MC's me and my boy's loved to listen to. I actually reached out to Little Dee first, we linked up made a track for his mix tape and became mates. When it came to my birthday bash that year I hollered at Little's about the OG.z coming down and doing a set and that was the first time I met Blacks and P Money.

I know P is a busy man. He smacks up the festivals, his own P.A's and Dub Step sets. He's that guy when it comes to the live circuit. He really puts in work. So when I hollered at him about jumping on this track I wasn't sure if he would have time to do it. After he heard the beat, he hit me back saying he was down and that he would record it ASAP. A man of his word, and a testament not only to his talent but how he handles his business, the verse was in my inbox around a week later. And he shut it down...

'Don't bother me with this lame bredda, who's thick as shit, saying he's sick ah, shit ain't even sick it's just shit see, I don't need a doc to tell me that you ain't better'.

That's how a beast on the mic jumps on a tune and proceeds to stamp his authority all over it. As the drums kick in P goes to town on any doubters and anyone gassed up thinking they are something they are clearly not. The verse brings back classic memories of P Money and the hours we spent listening to his music on the motorways up and down the country. I say hours we spent which isn't accurate as I still put classic P tracks like 'If A Man's Talking' and 'Hot One's' on compilation CD's for these road trips and they still have the effect that did when we were new to P Money's music back in the day. A true professional and a trained assassin on the microphone, it isn't hard to see why P Money is one of the most successful and prolific MC's in the UK in recent times. Big ups to P for completing the cycle and making '4 Lions' one of my favourite collaborations I have been involved with.

As a lover of sequel's and getting as much out of a good idea as I can I can definitely see life in the '4 Lions' concept. It doesn't have to end here as long as producers continue to send me fire and there are hungry MC's who want to tear into a track and rip the insides out of it.

Watch for the remix...

Month Eight

No Long Ting Featuring Ratlin

'No Long Ting, I ain't on a long one, bottle after bottle so ya done know were on one, looking at me funny blood I think you got the wrong one, don't lock off this party I just wanna hear my song run!'

The nod factor in our world is a particular ingredient that we always look for in our musical recipe when we're cooking up tracks. People talk about the lyrics, the flows and the hooks, but when you first hear a record it's usually the beat that pulls you in. As a kid I would run around all the specialist record shops on a Saturday with my boy Mista Driscoll, searching for the latest albums and 12 inch releases. As the guy in the shop would draw out the vinyl's and drop the needle into the groove of the record it was the nod factor among the Hip Hop junkies in the shop that would guarantee a sale of a record or not. If the groove of the beat was strong enough to get everyone's head nodding to the rhythm of the record, then it would get the thumbs up before the MC even started to spit. There have been conceptual records made about this, the most well-known being 'Busta Rhymes' 'Break Your Neck' but also a more rare and coveted one from 'Mad Skillz' aptly titled 'The Nod Factor'. Often at Hip Hop shows and live showcases, heads will line up on a dance floor to hear MC's do their thing. But they are not there to dance. Apart from slight body movements the common thread among the sea of Hip Hop followers is the way they nod their heads in time to the beats being played on the stage. An important part of crafting your music and knowing what they like is trying to supply them with the nod factor. As a rapper, I often do the nod test myself when I'm sent beats but the best way to do it is in a busy studio full of heads and see how they react to the beat you throw on. If they carry on talking, make mild gestures of appreciation or worse still remain motionless the beat or track you're playing will probably have the same effect on the audience. However, if all the heads in the studio start swaying back and forth in a hypnotic almost trance like fashion and fists are suddenly being thrown up to yours then you know you're onto a winner. People in the music industry often refer to the 'grey whistle test' which I believe relates to an A&R guy at a label playing tracks around the office to test them out on employees. If the tea lady walks up and down the office whistling a certain song the A&R man believes it's a sign of him having a hit record on his hands. Well, you can't whistle Rap so the good old fashioned 'grey whistle test' is useless to us. We know we have a track that's gonna do some damage in our world if it passes the 'Nod Factor' test. And when I played the beat for 'No Long Ting' in the studio it passed with flying colours.

I always like to work with new producers and one thing I always do is check out anyone who sends me beats. It can help if they've worked with some respected names and their CV is strong but on the whole it's all about how the beats sound when you press play. If you choose to stick to the producers you know and are comfortable with I believe you could be missing out on some diamonds in the dirt so I always keep my ears tuned to the streets and make an effort to source out new production. 'Kaze Beats' manager had sent me a link to a bunch of beats and as I went through them I was impressed with the production and the vibe he was coming with. I love those Trappy beats with attitude by the skip load and 'Kaze' certainly isn't lacking when it comes to evoking these types of feelings in the music he makes. When I heard the intro of 'No Long Ting' it was one of those magic moments where the writer makes the connection with the production. I can remember it like it was yesterday if I'm honest as I was still in bed. I decided to work on some music that morning and began to go through the tracks on Kaze's Sound Cloud from the moment I woke up. I can remember thinking that I didn't want any distractions so the best way to stay one hundred percent focused on getting some work done was to stay in bed and not get out and deal with the outside world till I had a full track written. As soon as I heard this particular beat I was on a vibe. The first lyric came easily. 'I ain't inna long ting, I ain't inna long talk'. There it was, I had my title and my concept. I like titles that come from every day talk. If someone sends me a tune and I like it I may say 'yeah I'll deal with that, no long ting'. I like using slang and terminology that the audience can relate to and use on a daily basis, so the hook or story line of the song resonates with them and they feel like the language used is relevant to them.

As soon as I had my first few bars written, I was in the zone. I quickly realized this track wouldn't be restricted by a strict concept and that it was more the feel of my flows that would carry it. When the beat switched I went from a slow hypnotic flow to a quicker paced rendition of bars. Some would say this is a style that Meek Mill has pioneered and made popular but I think I still put my own spin on it in terms of delivery and flow patterns. I'm not adverse to borrowing flows sometimes anyway. It's all part of the game, as long as your bringing your own flows to the table, then you're entitled to dip into someone else's pot and flip some of their flows. I don't mind when people do it with mine but if a rapper only copies and doesn't innovate then he or she is merely a karaoke artist.

Content wise my first verse isn't one of my deepest verses and I'll be the first to admit that, but it is honest. Ever since I was a young kid, I've enjoyed what our generation knows as 'getting on it'. I can remember being twelve or thirteen, drinking Thunder Bird, TNT Cider and super strength Lager. I've dashed the Thunder Bird and the strong Cider to the side but I still enjoy the rush of the odd Special Brew and I do enjoy a good drink. I've experimented with various substances throughout my life and although I don't smoke anymore I used to love weed. I struggle with staying on the straight and narrow which is why I 'never say never'. I have a demon on my shoulder and an angel in my ear. Most of the time the clear thinking and righteous nature of the angelic figure wins the day but every now and again I give up to the demon and go on a rampage. My friends have coined various names for this alter ego who lives inside of me. Back in the day they named him 'Vermin' and more recently he has morphed into 'the rascal'. To say this character is a handful would be quite an understatement so I keep him in the box most of the year. However, every now and again at house parties, my birthday or traditionally at Nottinghill Carnival I release him for the day. These day's he only comes out for a 24 hour period tops in comparison to the weekend benders of the past and I don't normally unleash him on the unsuspecting general public. The wave can be serious and you have to know how to work the surfboard to sit at the table. This beat had me on that edge and created pictures in my head of various hazy memories of these types of scenarios so I decided to rap about having a good time and record lyrics that would be loosely based around these themes.

I decided I would keep the hook for this song on that party vibe. That's why there are some almost cliché lines in there that people can easily sing along to and relate to. It's rare that I write with the club in mind but this is a fun record so I decided to keep it simple. I nearly changed the 'bottle after bottle' line but then I thought why hide from the truth. When the 'rascal' is out to play it's all about necking bottle after bottle, and a lot of young people in my audience can probably relate to that too. So for once I kept the hook aimed at people in the parties, having a good time and enjoying themselves. The game is all about balance and I believe my mix tape needed this balance. Also, going back to the essence of what this tape is about, it is supposed to represent my life over that period. And although I don't party as hard as I used to I definitely had my moments over the year where I went in. 'No Long Ting' is my fun party record of a ridiculous production from Kaze Beats where I got to let me hair down a bit and get wavy with a bottle of 'Grey Goose'.

One artist I knew I wanted on this tape from its early days of production was Ratlin. I've got a lot of love for this guy. I can remember him coming down to my birthday bash that year to rep and us performing together when I was on a wavy one. Ratlin is one of those real individuals in this game, a man of principals and a certified artist. We had linked up at 1xtra's 10th birthday celebrations up at the legendary Maida Vale Studios earlier in that year. Semtex had recruited a bunch of MC's including myself, Sneakbo, No Lay, Sincere, Scrufizzer, Ratlin and more to perform a live track on air called 'Ten Plus' saluting 1xtra's tenth year in the game of broadcasting. After the show we took a load of promo photos together and I chatted with Ratlin about collaborating on something. He beat me to it a few weeks later and asked me to jump on a track from his forthcoming mix tape 'Crown Me'. A guitar infused track with a powerful Rock chorus entitled 'Walking Wounded' which Charlie Sloth called 'Epic'. I was a real fan of the tape in general. I loved the collaboration records with 'Squeeks' and 'Blade Brown' but often found myself blazing Ratlin's solo tracks like 'The Streets Don't Love Me No More' and 'Roly'. After having the tape on constant rotation for a good month I sent Ratlin the beat for 'No Long Ting' as I could imagine his tone of voice sounding sick over the track. He was feeling it and within a week or so I had another bomb in my mail box. I loved the subtle aggression in the bars and the 'we ain't having it' attitude with purveyed throughout the sharp and distinctive delivery. As he rapped 'Harry tell this little rapper how a bigger boss lives, Champagne on the stage or up in the cockpit' I believed him. Another rapper could have spat that very same line and I wouldn't have. With Ratlin he delivers his lyrics with such authority, you can tell he means every single word he says. It isn't for effect or just to get you gassed, this is his life told through the art of bars. As he ends his verse saying he's 'nice with the word play but I'm nicer sitting outside where your bird stay' the authenticity shines through. The best in West came saw and conquered, nothing long.

On my last verse I decided to up the gears with my flow and come with some more complex double time patterns. I also chose to return to the basics of emceeing in terms of content. Brush the dirt off the shoulders and stake my claim as one of the nicest out here. It's a familiar and tried and tested subject matter in Hip Hop but it is always necessary. This is what makes us different to singers. A real MC always wants to go out to show why he or she is the best. He or she may make great songs for the radio but at the same time you have to go at the competition now and again and show you can really rap. Kendrick Lamar recently sparked this debate with his now legendary verse on Big Sean's 'Control' record where he named the hottest rappers in the American scene and told them he's trying to murder them and take their fan base. It wasn't anything personal and those of us who understand the culture that Hip Hop was built on didn't take any offence. Every time you record a verse you are supposed to be going all out to prove that you're the dopest out and outshine everyone else in the race. This is normal but Kendrick bought this ideology back into the forefront of the game which I think is good. I'm not the type of MC that chooses to do this on every record but it felt right on the last verse of 'No Long Ting'. So I took shots at snails in the game moving too slowly. I rapped about the props given to me on line by one of the best battle rappers in the business, Murda Mook. I even delved into boasts of minor wealth with the line 'so many garms when I open my cupboard up'. Of course me being me and not wanting to sound like I place too much worth and importance on material possessions I immediately rebuffed stating 'straight mad ting but I ain't Instagramming it'. But before you know it I'm back on my bullshit proudly calling myself a DNB Don with 'three awards in the cabinet'. It's a fun boastful and shamelessly braggadocios verse not to be taken too serious. Sometimes an MC just wants to big up his achievements on a record and this is what I chose to do here.

Month Nine

Monsta Featuring Flexplicit

*'I'm frankly Frankenstein, monster defined by the factual facts
in my rhymes, I created a beast in the lines my scripts are like
screenplay's, vivid imagery that's rarely seen this days'...*

I can remember how the whole 'Monsta' track came about like
it was yesterday. It was towards the end of February and I had
just dropped the 'Shuttin Em Down 'video featuring Dreps on
SBTV. A couple days after it went up on the channel I got a
bunch of DM's from Flexplicit on twitter about how the track
had inspired him to write a hook for me and to look out for it
in my mailbox. I had never met Flex before but I had caught
his videos with Mic Righteous, Royce Da 5 9 and Papoose so
I knew this guy was about his business. True to his word a
track arrived in my E Mails very quickly but I couldn't check
it straight away as I was away at the time. The fact he got it to
me at such a rapid pace made me realize how on point he was
when it came to making things happen. I can remember Flex
being on to me about checking it ASAP so as soon as I got
home; I jumped on the lappy and downloaded the track which
he had named 'Monsta'.

As the opening bars of the track kicked in I was intrigued
so turned it up a little louder. Just as I adjusted the volume
Flex's hook kicked in. I was expecting the unexpected but the

impact this chorus had on me coupled with the atmospheric production from AK blew me away. Some hooks are cool, some are wack, some are corny and come are plain epic. Flex had heard something within 'Shuttin Em Down' that inspired this monster of a hook and had decided to give me that fire. Some artists wouldn't do that; they would build a hot hook and decide to keep it for themselves. I had to respect Flex for putting something so powerful on the table and within minutes I was on the phone to him discussing the track and giving him the utmost respect for putting it my way. As we spoke on the phone I realized Flex is just one of those guys with a good heart. Some artists resent other artists with talent. Other's feel inspired by it and want to collaborate for the greater good of the music. Flex is one of these people. There are a lot of snaky individuals in the music business and it's refreshing when you connect with talented artists that you also get on with on a personal level. I also admired how quick Flex was with putting it together and sending it to me. One of my pet hates is chasing up rappers for verses or producers for beats. None of this was a problem with Flex; he was the one bugging me to make something happen with it! I had a good feeling about this record so I invited Flex down to the studio I was using at the time to record his parts. In the meantime the pressure was on me, I had to deliver on the verses. I asked Flex if he wanted a verse and he was like 'nah I'm cool with the hook, this is all about you'. As I listened to his hook where he say's 'if Britain needs a monster I'll take over the whole UK' I felt as though he was throwing down the gauntlet. I had to pick it up and beat the shit out of the beat and live up to the accolade that Flex was giving me in the chorus. If man is calling me a monster, I have to go extra hard with my bars. So the challenge was on... .

I absolutely love double time spitting. From Twista, to when I first heard Skiba and Shabba as a kid to guys like Scru Fizzer and Tech Nine today, I'm a fan of quick fire lyrics, tongue rolling and high powered double time delivery. I loved how Bone Thugs combined the skill of fast and furious flows with melodies. I can remember early Destiny Child records where Beyoncé would use some of the techniques in her vocal arrangements to great effect. One of my favourite MC's Jay Z always had a knack for this particular flow and in his early days of getting in the game it was what separated him from the crowd. It's also something I found I was quite adept to so it's always been part of my armoury as an MC. I can remember myself and Skiba pushing each other to the limits on tracks like 'Giddy Up' and 'Fire Bars 1' and of course the way me, Skibz and Fun would bounce off each other at 170 beats per minute on our Drum B N Bass mix tapes. I wanted some of that energy on the verses for 'Monsta' so rather than write a traditional Rap style flow I went back to my trusted double time roots and began to 'deal with the matter'.

> 'Word from the sponser, Flex came with a hook for the
> monster, man know about me up North, said he came
> in the game with Skibz and Funsta'.

Physiologically I guess this is me showing some love and props before I go into eating up the track. I had to big up Flex for what he had bought to the table, I wanted the audience to know this is something he has bought for me to devour. Acknowledgement and giving props is more important to me than anything else so it's also why I mentioned Fun and Skibadee. Back when I burst into the DNB scene in 2008 it was those guys who really helped me out a lot so I think it's only right to tilt my snapback to the people who have had a part to play in developing this particular 'beast on the mic'. The rest of the verse pays homage to my meteoric rise in the Drum N Bass scene and what can arise from this. 2008 was a crazy year for me, it was that year that the sleeping giant awoke and the 'monster' I speak of on this record began to become visible to the world. I was doing mixtape after mixtape with the crew, performing every weekend and I had started to upload videos of me spitting to Drum N Bass aswell as Rap on my You Tube channel. I quickly realized that I had to up my game. I had flows and an abundance of lyrics but my voice sometimes didn't sound as loud as the pioneers in the scene who had been rinsing out raves for years. I had to get in the gym, study what mic's the other MC's were using and work on my stage techniques. I was in at the deep end and it was time to sink or swim. I had to transform from a rapper who could spit double time into a Drum N Bass MC. But not just any Drum N Bass MC. I wanted to be up there as a favourite with your Eks Man's, Trigga's and Skibadee's. To rank alongside these guys would take a lot of focus and I fully immersed myself in the scene and worked hard to put myself in the position I am today.

I was so on my game that I started to see friends less. I was spending every second I could writing lyrics, performing or sleeping. My real mates didn't mind as they knew I had strived for years and I had to take the 'bull by the horns' so to speak and go all out to establish myself as face in the music scene. The opportunity provided by my long-time friend 'Funsta' couldn't be taken lightly and I had to take my shot. No one really started hating on me to my face but a couple sly comments said in jest were enough to let me know the 'streets were talking'. That's why I rap about it in the first verse of this track. We have a disease in Britain where we hate success. This country will back you when you're the underdog on your way up but when you reach any level of success they will try their hardest to bring you back down. This is where you have to go into monster mode and not be effected by hateful comments on the streets or on line. You have to feed off it and use it as your energy to keep going at it even harder. As I rap on the track, 'when you start blowing even your own people start hating'. The same bredda's who loved you off when you were struggling to pay your rent are quick to diss you for 'changing' when you're moving into a nice new place and are buying a few expensive clothes. Instead of being happy for you and knowing you have worked hard for this the old green eyes monster often comes into play as you rise in any walk of life. It's all part of the process though, so as I say on the song you have to know when to 'cut the dead weight' and not have negative energy around you that can suck you dry and ultimately bring you down to their level.

The second verse of the song features references to monster's such as Frankenstein and I go out to embellish the track with complex flow's and lyrical dexterity. I'm having a bit more fun on this verse. I've given props and respect to Flex and my elders and I've dealt with hatred and reaction to success so now I'm just gonna unleash the monster within. I speak of my versatility and my love for spitting at different tempo's and I also take shots at anyone trying to box me into a particular style. I try to build flows on top of flows as the record builds to the third verse and the final verbal assault.

As the drums break out to an almost accapella style section, I slow down my flow to create a feeling of calm before the storm. This is a technique I learnt from Drum N Bass records where they break down to simplicity before erupting in a chaotic drop. Carrying on with the monster theme I acknowledge that I believe many rappers fear me as strong competition in the game and perhaps there have been moves made to block me from reaching higher heights. As the lyrics on the song say 'took a look around they don't want me in this industry, so they pray that I go away that's not likely I must be a threat. It's a feeling I've felt over the years and I'm not ashamed to admit it. Even Semtex from 1xtra has stated on air that he thinks other rappers fear me. I can honestly say I don't fear anyone. This is why I'm so comfortable bigging up other rappers on line, tweeting links to buy their music and promoting their You Tube videos. However, sometimes the favour isn't returned and this is usually due to insecurity or fear. Much in the same way a child fears a monster as its something he feel's threatened by I feel some rapper's fear competition. So I touch on this issue as I believe it is something that isn't just relevant to me but to the whole scene and how we progress in the future. I've heard stories about rappers laughing and cracking jokes when other rappers are dropped from labels. This isn't something to be glad about as we should be rising as a scene together with some solidarity but everyone secretly wants to be the 'one' to blow.

Of course a monster isn't concerned with these childish notions so as the beat kicks in I go into a passionate tirade about change, switching up the rules, the real maintaining over the fake and opening up new lanes for the next generation to step into. Some may say these notions are idealistic but music can change people's perceptions and I am to this day amazed at how our words can affect people. This is why I personally choose to bring content and something relevant into my bars, even on a track like 'Monsta' which is essentially about me staking my claim as a beast on the mic. I prefer to end on a positive note, I want the audience of young kids listening to believe they can achieve and attain that monster status. We've all got that monster in us, whether we hide it under our bed like Rihanna or we keep it restrained within our personalities like myself. It's always there, ready to burst out and that's exactly what happened on this particular track.

Month Ten

The Epidemic Featuring Proverbz

'We search for courage as we try to fill these empty pockets, I'm always out there pinching pennies from the devils wallet, forever wandering this desert in the search for knowledge, we see the madness of the journey not the purpose of it'- Proverbz

When I first heard the beat to what became 'The Epidemic' I was taken back to the feelings and the emotional connection I had with those early Wutang albums. There is a nerve that the RZA was able to touch before any of those incredible mic titans even touched the track on those records that has been untouched in Hip Hop since. Whatever the RZA had in his mind, body and soul he was able to channel that energy and throw it into a production soundscape that was like nothing we had heard before. 'Redskull' to me is one of the best Hip Hop producers I have worked with as his music always brings out a kneejerk reaction in me thus bringing out some of my most personal or insightful writing. On some instrumental's you can have fun with flows and keep subject matter light hearted but with a lot of Skull's productions the beats are too intense to do that. You have to match the depth and substance in the production with something equally profound and compelling to the listener on the microphone. Take 'Hands Of Time' on my last mixtape 'Moonlight Hustle' for an example. I heard the strings at the beginning of the song and immediately began to reminisce about a friend I had lost due to tragic circumstance years ago. I wrote that particular record in about an hour as the music enabled me to release feelings I had kept locked away for many years. His music unearths pains and deep emotional feelings inside of me as a writer that would be swept under the carpet or relinquished if I didn't have the right productions to release them on. I am very thankful to him for the beats he has shared with me, thus allowing me to share my innermost thoughts with you the listener.

The beat on 'The Epidemic' is very special to me. It's everything I love about Hip Hop. It isn't about a catchy hook with a top line chorus to capture day time play. It isn't about any kind of gimmick or 'follow fashion' sound. It's the essence of Hip Hop in all its splendour and glory and it should be celebrated and held in high regard. A lot of people can make beats. Studying a current sound or emulating what is popular in the charts or on the dance floor is a simple formulaic process. To forge original sounds that people try to copy is not so easy. And to create vivid pictures in someone's head just through sound shows real talent. I felt I had these unique elements with this particular instrumental so it was a blessing but I knew I had a big task on my hand to make my lyrics marry such a perfect beat. The first thing I thought to myself was I needed to talk sense on this record but not just come with a bunch of conscious Rap clichés that the audience had heard a thousand times before. So I did what I often do when I comes to writing to a Skull production. I waited till night fall, poured myself a little Brandy and Coke and tried to lose myself in the instrumental slipping in and out of the songs melodies and drum patterns with various flows and ideas circulating through my mind. The first thing I thought about was control. I may have mentioned already that I am not a person who likes to feel pressured by society or any figure of power to succumb to their standards or way of life. As someone who uses social networks I have seen patterns of behaviour change on these forums so I thought about the way these tools often control us. When I first got my Black Berry I was addicted to it. Whether it was BBM, reading my @s on Twitter or replying to E Mails straight away I wouldn't put that phone down. It became glued to my hand and even during films I watched or nights out with my girlfriend I would have to take regular looks at my phone to see if I had missed anything. In a sense I became a slave to the technology and in turn conversation and real interaction with those around me suffered. As the beat played I thought about this and how many people, young and old are now glued to their phones, scrolling down their Facebook time lines to see what people in their contact list are up to. If someone writes 'feel so mad right now' the friends of this person write back underneath the said status to add support or comfort to the friend in need. Back in the day that person would have gone to see a mate at the pub to talk through their problems, made a telephone call to a close friend to discuss it or reached out to their partner or a family member about it. Now we sit on the couch at home, phone in hand and share our frustrations with the world enjoying the attention and traffic it brings to our page. It began to rekindle my hatred of control no matter how passive and the more I thought about it the more it became transparent that to a certain extent these social networks are controlling our lives. Worse still they can become destructive and divide communities as everyone voices there often extremist opinions on their Twitter or Facebook accounts. We then have a classic case of civil unrest and hatred that trickles into the streets in which we live fuelled by comments and arguments put across on the popular social networking web sites. With all this in mind I was fully fired up and began to write my first bar of defiance.

'They'll never draw me into their agenda on a social network, give everyone a voice to spout their ignorance, familiar tactics and tools their using for divide and conquer use the internet to their advantage giving

power to a plonker with extremist views, whatever happens they win, we lose, set the fire these opposing sides don't wanna diffuse'.

As I delved deeper into the thought process I threw a couple darts at the keyboard warriors who often hide behind these sites, disrespecting from the comfort of their desk, trolling and bullying others as they believe they are safe from any comebacks. But this has been spoken about before and I didn't want to waste too much time tackling familiar subjects. So I thought about the forums and the Facebook status's I had seen that had created heated arguments over sensitive subjects. It's often easy to get drawn into these debates you feel passionate about on line and I have been guilty of it myself in the past. But it really doesn't change anything. A lot of the time it only adds to a problem as individuals who are from opposing sides of the fence don't calmly debate their differences to find solutions. They merely end up in a war of words which often ends up in a slagging match of childish name calling, thus adding more animosity and hatred to an already volatile situation. This is why I say 'you won't catch me on line involved in any debate, that divide our streets and only guarantee more hate'. Hopefully I can heed my own advice in the future but nobody's perfect and I'm sure I'll say something stupid after one too many one night on the road that will offend someone. We are after all humans with all the imperfections and blemishes that come with that and we don't always have to agree. This is what led me to my next stream of thought where I talk about not hating someone or their music just because I don't personally choose to listen to it. A lot of rappers and particularly up and coming artists get very emotional if you don't co-sign their music on line. I'm honestly someone who tries to listen to all the links people send me. But I'm not going to big it up and call it the best thing since sliced bread if I honestly don't feel it. If I retweet everyone's music and big up every single artist who sends me stuff then it won't mean anything when I co-sign an artist, mixtape or music video I feel is worthy of it. The internet is a gift and a curse in that sense anyway. It's now completely saturated with artists as everyone now has that window to showcase their music. Which is cool to an extent, but there has to be standards and it has to mean something if you reach the levels of getting your music on respected sites like SBTV, Link Up TV and GRM Daily. So if I don't retweet your music or big up everything you send me it isn't because I hate it or you as an artist it's because I want my opinion to mean something to people when I really get behind an artist or big up a particular mix tape or visual on line. People like me often watch the progress of artists, so you could be shooting yourself in the foot if you don't get the reaction you expected from your first release and choose to dis an on line forum or an artist or DJ because you feel they are not supporting you. It sometimes takes four or five videos or songs before you start to garner up support and generate heat. So just work hard, keep grafting and don't get too emotional as it may affect your opportunities in the future.

Another thing I decided to go into on this record was the blatant lack of respect the UK music industry and a lot of the general public have for the art of rapping. One of the reasons I chose to write this book was to give people an insight into the process of writing a mix tape or a Hip Hop album and how much work and how much of our soul we pour into projects like this. People's perceptions of how we put together our music and the real craft that goes into being a good MC is not really understood therefore not respected in my opinion. Take X factor for example. Not the coolest thing to admit but I always watch it every year. One thing I noticed on recent episodes of the programme is they have absolutely no understanding of what separates a good rapper from a bad one. All they know is its cool and they realize through the likes of Eminem and Jay Z invading pop culture is that it's very popular and influential on today's generation. So without being disrespectful to previous contestants they hear very amateur nursery rhyme raps with poor breathe control executed with zero passion or power and say 'I love the Rap'. If a singer came into that audition and delivered a vocal of the same quality as the rap they claim to love they would send them packing. This is why I rap 'they understand a technical singer like Minnie Ripperton but they don't understand the skill factor and type of rappers they inspired me to kick the rhymes I'm kicking em'. Where they have no affinity with Hip Hop and no knowledge of the art form they really can't comment on it or give any constructive feedback. This parallels the offices of A&R men in the UK who often have zero understanding of what makes an MC incredible which is why some of the best are side-lined in favour of whatever rapper or so called Urban act a manager they know brings to their attention. There are deeper theories of why the art form of Rap but more so the culture of Hip Hop isn't respected, but is often ridiculed in this country. Some argue that due to people's prejudices and supressed racism they have a phobia of the attitude that comes with the music. They don't want their children's jeans to sag and their offspring littering there vocabulary with street slang. They frown on white kids adopting black phrases, wearing hoodies and terrorizing their homes with bass heavy Hip Hop full of curse words and themes they deem sexist from their own perspective. So in this country they laugh at Rap and all its achievements. The mainstream media actively try to bring down acts like 'N Dubz' who hail from the streets, and replace them with more palatable rapping artists like 'Macklemore' who raps about things that were often unacceptable in the culture of Hip Hop. And whilst an artist like 'Kendrick Lamar' who represents everything that is great about being an MC is snubbed at the Grammys, 'Macklemore' walks with four of the prestigious awards.

Before I knew it I had written to half of the beat, acknowledging my own faults and subscriptions to consumerism but also endeavouring to be a better person I finished the verse with some multi syllable flows and felt I had said everything I wanted to say. I could have ended the track at two minutes thirty seconds, but I felt like another voice had to come on and speak from their perspective. This voice had to be correct for the song though. Even the tone of the guest had to be perfect. This beat to me was one of my favourites on the mixtape and I was satisfied with my attack on it so the voice I added to the mix couldn't detract from what we had so far, it had to add to it and lift it to another dimension for the second part of the record. It had to make sense. It had to be just right.

'It's mad how this shit became an epidemic, these people so brainwashed they don't seem to get it, they don't understand or ever see the symptom spreading'...

As Proverbz touches this track it reminds me why I love Hip Hop so much. It triggers back memories of the magic of the UK rappers I grew up on like Klashnekoff, Skinny Man and Task Force. It is testament to the sort of rappers who inspired me to pick up a pen and put my thoughts on an A4 piece of paper rather than keep them bottled up. His tone is magic and the words flow like wine. Its poetry in motion, a demonstration of the brilliant wordsmiths I speak of in my verse. There are rappers who make records that gas me up and I enjoy listening to on the road. There are rappers who make great songs for the clubs. There are rappers who try to kick knowledge but just spout clichés and bore us with sentiments we've heard a million times before. And then there's rappers like Proverbz. Rappers who have the ability to marry the music and weave in and out of the track with compelling flows, rhyming schemes and make you think without preaching to you. I love rappers who have a vast vocabulary and who pepper the beat with interesting language and break down subjects in different ways. Proverbz is one of these rappers. I was thrilled to get him on this track as I can remember finishing my verse and only hearing him next. If he wasn't down for it, I would have probably ended the song at that point. I couldn't really hear anyone else on the track so I would have been going for a second best putting anyone else other than Proverbz on the song. He was actually the last person to send his feature back. We were getting close to the deadline of mixing down the whole tape and he just got it over in time. But it was worth its weight in gold.

This is actually one of the songs I am most proud of in all my years of making music because I think the three of us really took all our talents to new heights and produced something we can all be proud of. As a kid these are the kind of tracks I wanted to make. Regardless of industry trends and shifts in how the music is marketed I will always endeavour to write music like this. Even if these aren't the songs that are my most successful commercially these are the moments I make music for. I can't betray my heart or my natural passion for the artistry of Hip Hop in all its essence which I think is what we represented with great pride in 'The Epidemic'.

Month Eleven

'Super Calm'

'We keep it calm, no hype talk understand, I bring the logic to the game, them man are Garage Band'

I like messing about with different tones and experimenting with my voice sometimes. In terms of vocal delivery the mood of the production really guides me in this area and every now and again I'm played a beat where I know I will be able go a bit left of centre with my attack. For me, it just keeps it fresh, especially on a project like 'Twelve Month's where I'm holding down eighteen tracks. Singers and guest vocalists obviously add spice and variation to a project but I don't think artists should be afraid to step outside their comfort zone and try new things themselves. I can't hold a note when it comes to singing for instance. But every now and again I try melodic sing songy choruses in the comfort of the studio booth and now and again it works. It doesn't matter when it doesn't because at least I'm pushing the envelope and trying new things. Artists who always 'play it safe' don't seem to last long in my eyes as audiences are quite fickle and can become bored with the same formula's. When you think about artists who have lasted decades as opposed to years it's because they have moved with the times, tried new things and reinvented their sound on numerous occasions to keep themselves relevant.

When I heard the beat for 'Super Calm' I knew immediately that this was going to be one of those tracks I could get a little quirky with. I had linked Red Skull in Stevenage as I was running some MC Workshops in a school nearby. We were posted up by the train station and Skull was playing me a selection of his new instrumentals. Upon hearing the bassline and the shuffling drums I was sucked in to the production, which became 'Super Calm' immediately. It's always a good sign when I start to formulate flows in my head straight away. Sometimes I don't know what the concept of the song is going to be but I can hear flows and patterns. I had an instant connection with the production on this track. The instruments Skull had used and the switches in the song provided a gateway to new and exciting flows so I knew this would be a track I would have to write to. It didn't sound like a Timbaland or a Missy Elliot track but the vibe of it reminded me of some of my favourite tracks from them in terms of the track's dynamics and the 'out of the box' approach to the production. I used to love the way Missy's tracks were arranged and how she always came with a left field attack on the microphone. I actually don't think Missy gets enough credit for what she bought to the game, musically and visually. But that's another story!

I took the 'Super Calm' beat away on a CD and started to write to it as soon as I got in. It wasn't like any of the beat's I had written to before and that's saying something as I've written a lot of tunes. What this beat blessed me with was the perfect opportunity to rap differently on it. Calm is probably not how people would describe my delivery normally. Fiery, aggressive, passionate and energetic are adjectives I've heard used to describe my particular vocal style. So I decided to fully go against that, step outside of the box and try something new. I will come with my trademark double time patterns but I will rap them in a much cooler calmer tone rather than the abrasive style I'm known for. The word that kept coming in my head was 'calm' which in turn gave me the concept for the song. It would not only keep my style a little calmer and laid back but this would ultimately give me the content for the track.

I began to think about scenarios and situations in my life where I have found it more beneficial to remain calm and level headed rather than scream and shout and get nowhere. If you remain cool, calm and collected and analyse a problem rather than get too much emotional about it you can usually work the situation to your advantage. The music business is like a game of poker. You don't show everyone your hand until you want him or her to see it. And you only want them to see it when you have the winning hand. Just like any business this industry is full of people who are looking to take your place and it can get very political. When things get political emotions creep in, people get angry, voices are raised and insults are thrown. People fall out and a lot of the time they put their principals and pride above the growth of their business. I've found a calm voice of reason wins over anger every single time so as I began to write my first verse I had vivid images running through my head of people I've come across who run around like 'chickens with their heads cut off' looking very busy achieving very little. As I rap on my opening lyric 'I'm super calm, I'm super blessed, this guy on my line is super stressed, and I'm trying to get this guy off my line, gotta go and do a show in Budapest'. Negative vibes can really rob you of your energy so spending time on the phone with individuals who drain this energy is something you need to cut out if you want to achieve success. Some people go through life fighting every single injustice, causing problems everywhere they go, putting people's backs up. They become isolated, as they have destroyed relationships with most people around them, instead surrounding themselves with yes man who don't challenge their authority. I aim to remain calm around these characters when I am forced to deal with them but ultimately I aim to remove these suckers of energy from my circle in a calm manner.

People aren't used to a calm approach to situations. It freaks them out if they phone you flying off the handle with anger full of expletives and you answer them in a cool tone. If you aren't drawn into the emotion of the argument it almost looks like you don't care which can agitate a said individual. I try to stay calm with everything these days. I hope that doesn't mean I am suppressing rage and obviously I am human so I can't always keep my cool but I find that most things people get angry about really aren't worth it. Someone will tell me about something that has happened that has really pissed them off and although I smile politely, inside I wonder how this person would deal with a real problem in life if they were suddenly faced with it. This is why I rap 'wanna go another hood where they don't know me, face too bait now they think that I'm moany'. I'm not down for feeding into negative situations or beefs; it doesn't make me a moaner or someone who looks down on anyone. I just can't get involved in petty squabbles and hating on others when I'm trying to push myself to new limits as an artist and also be a better person. As a rap on the hook 'if you wanna bring me drama I just par a man' which means if you are a peddler of negativity and you carry that kind of energy with you I won't disrespect you. I will just calmly remove myself from your circle and tend not to be around you anymore. It's the 'super calm' approach to dealing with that situation. No arguments, no slagging mentions and certainly no on line 'twitter beef', Although I am guilty of finding it entertaining at times I would never publicly air any of my problems with someone on line which is why I finish the chorus saying no @'s fam better go and check your DM's. I don't believe in these altercations being public knowledge. It doesn't serve any purpose but to entertain those watching the time line getting off on the fact that we as artists or friends are dissing each other in the public arena. Some artists have used the on line beef's to their advantage and good luck to them but it isn't for me and I hope I never get sucked into it.

On verse two of the song I continue to lay into attention seekers who shout loud and talk a big game but yet again seem to just go round in circles. I talk about those so concerned with image and hyping up an almost gangster persona when they are really not about that life. I have been around people that are fully about that life, some of my good friends are. But I never have been myself so I don't try to fabricate an image I have to live up to that isn't true. If you put out that kind of energy and you can't back up your claims there are going to be people who want to see if your 'really about that life'. So as I rap on the song 'next time just keep it cool and hush your gums your not about that stuff you brag about and you boast about, you shout about and you talk about, its lies when I see them guys I'm Mick Dundee I went walkabout'. People are too quick to try and draw you into their beefs and problems with others. And half the time it's that classic scenario of two guys outside a club pushing each other but no one throwing a punch. It's all talk and rarely amounts to anything so is purely a waste of time and energy that could be put into more positive endeavours. Of course you have to 'ride with your people' but be mindful you're not 'Cee' in 'Bronx Tale' pressured into situations that could ultimately lead to your downfall. And over what? Most of the time it's a bunch of bullshit that really isn't worth fighting over and could end in seriously bad consequences. In the movie 'Bronx Tale' directed by Robert De Niro, the film's hero 'Cee' is pressured into riding with his childhood friends into a beef he really doesn't believe in. But he's in the back of the car, smiling and riding with his crew as he doesn't want to be seen as weak or someone who doesn't back up his friends. All he wants to do is get out the car and he eventually does, thanks to his mentor 'Sunny' who pulls him from a pool of self-destruction which could have ended in his demise. Obviously it's a fictional tale but the story line is something we can all relate to. I've been in situations over the years were I felt out of control in potentially dangerous settings but I learnt from it and endeavoured to not place myself in those settings again. It is said that the only real mistakes you make are the ones you don't learn from and I think there is a lot of truth in that.

The third verse starts off with some skippy flows to add another dimension to the track. Just like song's feature different sections to add spice and excitement in terms of bridges, harmonies or guitar solos I like to add these sections but vocally. Now and again I will keep the same flow through out a whole song but most of the time I aim to keep my flows changing throughout the duration of a track so the listener never knows what's coming next. I probably make it hard for myself but in doing this and going the extra length with my verses I feel I bring something unique to the game. Plus, people can copy or remix one flow but if you're doing ten flows in one song can they copy them all?

This particular track was fun to write. The whole idea of the 'Twelve Months' mix tape was to give the listeners an insight into my experiences, good or bad throughout the year. As I've said in previous chapters this year had definitely been an emotional rollercoaster and making songs like this where I just zone out and get lost in the music were very helpful to me. As much as this world continues to stress me out at times it's a blessing to be able to escape through the avenue of writing songs. In a sense it's a calming process and a great tool in my aim to remain 'super calm' in a world of chaos and confusion.

Month Twelve

Dance Move Freestyle

'Big Shots I don't skank in a rave, merc stage, two twos I'm back in the cave, get sleep, eat, sex then I'm back in a rave but I was a next yoot yeah back in the days'...

The original mixtapes I used to get as an avid Rap fan were very different to the modern day phenomena they have become now. Back in my school days they were very much DJ led with the likes of DJ Clue, Kay Slay and MK in the UK bringing together all the latest cutting edge tracks before they were released into the shops. Some DJ's would mix, scratch and make blends of the tracks whilst other's who were more personality led, would do shouts over the tracks and really play the exclusive card of being able to get hold of music before anyone else. I particularly liked the idea of the mixtapes as it wasn't so mainstream and would actively search out the latest tapes where I could find material that wasn't available on vinyl yet. I can remember me and my best mate Driscoll finding a mail order service in New York called 'Tape Kingz' and regularly getting the hottest mix tapes shipped over to us, thus staying ahead of others who would rely on import releases or tape new music off Westwood or 279's radio shows. By getting these tapes from the States we felt closer to the scene over there and were exposed to some great artists before they even got record deals.

I can remember when DJ's first started including freestyles on their tapes. One of my favourites was on a Mista Cee tape and featured Biggie Smalls before he had blown up. The intro had Biggie waxing lyrical over a smoothed out Blaxplotation backdrop before tearing into a remix of a Casual track with a vigour I hadn't heard in an MC in a long time. This inspired me to start drawing for my 12inch vinyl's out, plugging in my £15 microphone from Dixon's and recording my own freestyles. I still have some on tape and when listening back you can hear strong American influences but you have to start somewhere and at least I was developing my writing. Getting more and more tapes sent over from Tape Kingz, myself and Driscoll were particularly into tapes from Doo Wop. He had all the exclusives and dropped the most popular records but he had something other tapes didn't. His own squad of MC's from Harlem called 'The Bounce Squad'. I don't recall any of these rappers having record deals but they were raw with the bars. Doo Wop would throw on all the popular instrumentals of the time and they would eat into the beats like savages and conquering lions tearing up the tracks with a passion that was lacking in some of the signed rappers of the time. By the time the first official 'Bad Boy Records' tape dropped, me and Driscoll were addicted to the mixtape culture and this was one of our favourite tapes. Doo Wop had smashed it with his own squad but what Puffy did with this tape was different. It wasn't just talented yet quite unknown rappers rolling out freestyles; it featured the likes of Redman spitting new bars on popular tracks as well as exclusives from the Lox and other Bad Boy artists. I can't even tell you if Puffy was the first person to do a tape like this but I can whole heartedly say it was the first time I had seen or heard it done so well and it made a massive impact on me.

Its mad how mixtapes then began to evolve. Artists began to drop mixtapes to create a buzz in the streets and generate a fan base. Look at how 50 Cent and G Unit did it in New York. They flooded the streets with tapes featuring 50 and the crew rhyming on all the biggest instrumentals of the time and the buzz became so huge it ultimately led to Eminem becoming a fan of 50 through the tapes and signing him to Shady/ Aftermath. I can remember D Block killing the tapes too and although a tape would still be hosted by a DJ such as Whoo Kid or Drama the tapes were now a vehicle to create a buzz for an album, keep an artist hot in the streets or even get someone signed. I yet again was invigorated by these tapes, which were now released on a CD format and would seek them out in shops like Deal Real and Dark N Cold in London. I loved the idea of taking the hottest track at the time, killing it with your own bars and throwing it out there to the people. I put my own spin on this and instead of just releasing a mixtape I would record special versions of songs for DJ's on Kiss, Choice and Radio 1 which they loved and would play week in week out on their radio shows. Simply flipping a freestyle was how Semtex first noticed me. Lethal Bizzle had just dropped Pow 2011 and like most other people into the scene I was gassed!!! I had to get the instrumental and record my own version of it. When I did I put it up on You Tube and sent the link to a few DJ's. Sem heard it and asked for a clean version so I did it and headed out to Amsterdam for a show. Whilst I was on stage waiting to go on my twitter started to go crazy. Not only had Semtex played it on his legendary 1xtra show, he had reloaded it three times. Such accolades and props are not easy to come by and it was due to this freestyle that my relationship with Semtex developed into my weekly Rap Round Up slot on his show.

So as a fan of freestyles and someone who became known for putting my own spin on popular tracks such as 'Pass Out' 'Woo Riddim' and of course 'Pow 2011' I wanted to include at least one freestyle on this mix tape. My choice of instrumental wouldn't be obvious to some but if you understood how much me and my friend Brandalo listened to Mac and Cheese 3 by French Montana on our way to bookings that year it would become fully transparent. There is a track on their called 'Dance Move' that features one of my all time favourite rappers 'Fabulous'. We had this record on constant rotation on the motorways so when I heard the beat was available on an instrumental mix tape I immediately downloaded it and started to get busy.

The freedom a freestyle gives you in comparison to a track is endless. With a song you have to think about hooks, keeping the verses to a basic 16 bar structure and other constraints due to radio play. You don't have any of this when writing a freestyle. You can kick back, zone out with the beat and a glass of yak and put your heart and soul into the bars. I think this is why I've written so many of my best bars on freestyles. I just let go and fully experiment and I don't know where I'm going to end up. All I'm trying to do is shut down the beat and get all my thoughts out there, which is what I tried to do with the 'Dance Move Freestyle'. I'm not adverse to remixing flows for freestyles and flipping the original concept but on this one I wanted to bring my own double time flows to the table rather than spit like French or Fabulous and totally flip the subject matter.

In terms of lyrical content this beat almost put me in a trance whilst I was writing to it and I covered so many different topics starting off with my evolution from Drum N Bass raver to Drum N Bass MC. As I say on the track 'I picked up the mic and put down the weed, I see success I wanna know how it tastes'. Rolling over the production from 'The Renegades' I spoke of my days as a raver and the changes and sacrifices I had to make to transform from a partygoer into a professional MC. Don't get it twisted, I still party from time to time. It wouldn't be healthy not to but to really succeed in this business I think your drive and focus has to be maintained at all times and too much partying can be detrimental to that process.

Reminiscing about my lifestyle at the time led to more familiar braggadocios themes spiced up with a slew of metaphors and similes'. The main thing I found with this track as I got deeper into the writing was how relentless the flow was. People often ask me 'when do you breathe' whilst rapping and this freestyle has become a testament to skills I have learnt over the years in terms of breathe control. It has always annoyed me when singers try to rap mid-way into a performance as they often sound out of breathe when rapping. This is because most people don't understand some of the technical skills we as MC's have to harness over the years to become a good MC. Sure, I spit the classic line 'it's all about bars' but the way you deliver the bars is crucial. A flow can look great on a piece of paper but if you can't deliver it with any strength it's going to sound weak to the listener.

As the track builds up to the last minute I start to weigh in on friends who would rather hate than congratulate. It's a common theme in our genre but it's a familiar plot line to many rap records as haters are very real and as you rise you can expect to generate more hate. It's all a part of the business though and you mustn't let it get you down or deflate you. I've had members of my team or even family members get really offended when they see a spiteful comment about me but those types of comments don't bother me. In fact they actually help me as I often answer back in my bars and it gives me more material and therefore more output. If you use the hate in the right way it can actually help you win! Obviously I believe that getting hate means you are doing something right but everything has to be judged on its own merit and perspective. For instance if I have a video on You Tube and it has 500 likes and 20 dislikes I don't really have to pay attention to the dislikes as the majority are feeling it. If however I or another artist puts up a visual and it gets more dislikes than likes or even if the ratio is close you may have to rethink your strategy, admit that it wasn't good enough or perhaps it wasn't right for your audience. The internet is great for testing out product, just remember that not everyone is a hater and you have to differentiate between straight hate and constructive criticism.

The last point I choose to make on this freestyle relates to remixing flows. Now I personally believe that remixing flows from time to time is part of Hip Hop and there's nothing with it as long as you bring your own flows to the table and you give credit to the creator. If I hear a Kendrick track I like and I decide to remix his flow on a freestyle then I feel I can do that because for the most part I add innovation to the game through flow patterns I myself have invented. If however you ONLY take others flows you are violating. I remember when Meek Mill first came out. Every single up and coming rapper I heard for the next few months were jumping on his flow and trying to blow with it. Same with Skiba in DNB. I can recall running a number of workshops and kids openly biting not only Skibadee's flow but some of his lyrics too. This is why I used this song as a demonstration of how to jump on a Stateside production and totally bring your own flow to the beat. If you play my freestyle back to back with the original track by French Montana and Fabulous I sound nothing like them. As I rap on the song 'I'm an individual and my flow is original so I did my own flow on a French track, man borrow flows all the time we know that but if I was Ace Hood and they jumped on tracks with my flow getting them platinum plaques I'd be like dog better give that back'. In this case I used 'Ace Hood' as my example as at the time he was the rapper so many MC's were riding off in terms of flow. Some of these guys are big established rappers too. The reason I spoke about this is because it's quite dangerous in terms of the real originator of a flow losing credit for something he or she created. What can happen is an underground MC will come up with an exciting new flow pattern. He or she jumps on You Tube and drops freestyle with the said flow/rhythmic pattern. A bigger or more established MC will hear it and love it and remix it on his or her latest freestyle or track then the mainstream audience thinks this artist came up with the flow which is not correct.

As I end the freestyle I go out with a flurry of double time and call out the copy cats who ride off other people's flows or bars. I've always said that it's easy for people to steal flows, gimmicks or even lyrics but what they can never duplicate is my all round delivery and ability. I end the track with the following bars at a breakneck speed that would be hard to Xerox...

> 'You all know me I spit that crack it's going off when I hit that track, it's a fact I attack like a mac, never lack, bare shots going off and I will not slack, never that, pepper that, the berretta flows back, bare man wanna copy, try copying that'...

Case Closed...

Month Thirteen

Voices

'It's coming like I'm my own worst enemy, voices in my head conflict what their telling me'

They say hearing voices is one of the first signs of madness. If that's really true I should have been certified a long time ago. Ever since I was old enough to get some type of grip on the realities of life I've had voices in my head steering my decisions. And don't get it twisted I'm not talking about a deep rooted physiological problem here. I'm referring to the voices of wisdom I hear when I'm faced with a problem or an obstacle to overcome. Life is often referred to as a journey or a learning curve that never ends. On my journey I have learnt a lot from people around me. I've learnt how to work business situations to my advantage without upsetting people too much. I've learnt when to fight my battles and when to let certain shit slide. I've learnt about people's emotions and how they often get the better of them. I've seen how to execute a plan properly. And I've seen how you can easily mess everything up. This is why when I'm confronted with an issue I often hear voices in my head. I hear the tones of guys who would handle this situation in the wrong way and I see the consequences of their actions. Then I hear the voices of reason and the people who have been successful and I weigh up the situation and the best way to deal with it. I sometimes don't even hear the voice of someone I know. Due to the fact I enjoy reading and I'm pretty good at remembering information I care about I can sometimes relate the situation with someone I've learnt about through research. I'm presented with a problem and I immediately wonder what someone like Jay Z would do in this scenario? How would he deal with this problem and use it to his advantage? Life experiences of people are great when weighing up how to deal with something but having a vast knowledge of how successful people deal with similar scenarios can really help you to win and get the best out of tricky situations. The cliché of 'knowledge is power' is one I still believe in. It's how you use the knowledge that counts. For instance Nas read all kinds of books and even dictionaries front to back to expand his knowledge of language. He didn't do this because he was some kind of book worm. He did it so his vocabulary would be superior to other MC's of his age who would often used tired and tested words in their rhymes. Whilst other MC's would be happy to use the word 'head', Nas would prefer to say 'cranium'. I find the more words, voices, ideas and pieces of advice that you have flying around in that head or as Nas would say 'cranium' of yours the better decisions you'll make in life. If you get up in the morning, listen to Radio 1, read the Sun, go football on Saturday and keep a very limited group of friends from a similar cultural background I would suggest that the way you think about situations in life would be quite limited. I like to see both sides of an argument before I make my mind up about who is right. It could be that both people are right in their own way for example. Life is never that simple. This is when the voices in your head can start to get a little confusing.

I wrote 'Voices' at a time in my life when I was a bit confused myself. I had just lost my father. Losing any family member or friend is a testing time but when your mum or your dad passes away it makes you question a lot of stuff. When I heard the production for 'Voices' I wouldn't say I was in a bad way or low but I was definitely in a reflective mood.

I was thinking deeply about what really counts in life. For instance listening back to my one of my CD's from a couple years ago I had said 'money over everything' in a bar. What was I thinking? Money at this stage in my life meant nothing to me. But back then I was on the paper chase, trying to stack as much as possible I was always rapping about hustling hard and getting paper. My business mind kind of took control of my heart and what I was rapping about and maybe I lost sight of what was important. Money is something I still focus on as I have bills to pay but it certainly isn't a commodity you put over 'everything' and certainly not anyone. Losing someone close to you can really make you think about these things and how you handle problems you are faced with. You suddenly begin to hear voices and words of wisdom that you were numb to before as you have ascended to a different way of thinking. So when I sat down with this piece of production from 'Redskull' I envisioned myself on the top of a cliff overlooking a beautiful calm ocean and although I was still in my front room I felt like I was transported to that place through the music and I began to pour my feelings onto the page.

I didn't know I was going to call the song 'Voices' or have any great plan of what I wanted to say lyrically. I just knew there was a lot going on in my head and I had to pull it out and once again use music as my therapy.

As I wrote the first lyric I thought of all the things that life has thrown at me and how I have always fought against the negative energy and pushed forward to better myself. This music industry is full of ups and downs. Just when you think you're about to push up to a new level or sign with a label the knock back comes and you slide down the snake as quickly as you climbed the ladder. I have always been very thick skinned and not let these setbacks get me to down. Being a great believer in using a negative situation to your advantage I have always fought back twice as hard when something hasn't worked out in the way I wanted it to. I may retreat to regroup and come back stronger but I have never been a 'wounded animal' that sinks further into a sea of depression. So as I rapped my first line I spoke of this defiance and how they can 'throw it all it all at me' but I will 'throw it back and not accept it'. Questioning what someone says and not taking it lying it down is one of the reasons I'm still here doing my thing. If I listened to the negative voices over the years who have told me that 'it's impossible' or 'it's too late' I wouldn't be sitting at this computer writing these words right now. I have never given in and I never will. As I wrote this on my make believe cliff top I started to feel powerful through music again, thinking of all the madness I've had to overcome to get to where I want to be and all the things I have achieved against all the odds.

Thinking about all this made me analyse where I was in this stage of my life and at this point I can remember wanted to fly away into the sky and feel the freedom of the birds. My phone was ringing, I had a lot of texts and e mails to return and all I wanted to do was fly into the sky and leave it all behind. I wanted that freedom you only have as a child where you don't have a care in the world. I was getting agitated with people around me and I felt like I wanted to be alone. Maybe this is why I pictured myself alone on that cliff with the ocean below me. I started to question the success in the music game I had and the name I had built up. Did I really want it and all the bullshit that comes with it? As these thoughts ran through my mind I heard the voices of reason in my head. 'Now youv'e got it it's like you don't appreciate your gift, all you wanted was success when we was smoking in the lift'. I thought back to the days when I was living in a tower block overlooking the promenade in Gravesend and how much I yearned to be known for my bars, my ambition for success burning deep within me. We used to go to Drum N Bass raves and get gassed to Skibadee and Shabba. Now I was on the stages at the same raves getting the same love and respect for my lyrics and I was questioning whether I wanted to do it anymore? Why was I thinking like this? Music and particularly Drum N Bass had empowered me and given me my voice and an army of supporters. Why would I want to throw away everything I had worked for? As I asked these questions the voices in my head began to answer me...

> 'Now you've got it it's like you don't appreciate your gift, all you wanted was success when you was smoking in the lift'...

Then it hit me. Due to things going on in my life at the time I was trying to run away. It's a trait in humans that we see again and again. When things get confusing and what's really important starts to blur you often prefer to 'fly with the birds' or 'run away' rather than confront the issues head on and deal with them. Now I'm no therapist, but what I think I was trying to do was return to a place in my life where I didn't have these worries and concerns. I wanted to go back to the place where my father was still here, I didn't have all these texts and e mails to write, I didn't have the pressures of an audience watching me every weekend, studying my mixtapes and my lyrical content and in my head everything seemed more straight forward. I wanted to run away to the old block, get a bottle of Brandy and some weed, pull out the old CD packs and go raving on the weekend. I didn't have these problems or pressures to deal with in that place and some of these confusing voices seem to encourage me to go back there. Although I knew this was impossible I couldn't help but think I would be happier back in that life. Of course these notions were wrong. You can't turn back the hands of time and go back. That part of my life was a time to be enjoyed for what it was. People move on. I had moved on and just as I had in my past I had to step up again and confront my demons.

Moving into the second verse I started to feel a bit more clear headed and open to express myself. I thought about my feelings of trying to run away from my problems and realized how mad I would have been to have thrown away everything I have worked for. I closed my eyes and I was back on that cliff, the oceans waves swirling below me, the beauty of nature all around me. I now began to appreciate the simple things that we take for granted every day. Fresh air, the stars at night, the makeup of the human body, the love of family and friends. I could see that ocean and that sky with the full moon and the stars shining and things started to become clear. I thought of my struggles and all the sacrifices I had made. I thought about my mum and all the things she's done for me. I thought about my early memories of my dad, the good times we had shared. I thought about my manager Dave, our journey together and the fact he had never given up on me. I thought of my friends, I thought of my beautiful fiancée and I thought about the people who wrote to me online or who had come up to me in raves saying my music meant something to them. As I got deeper with my thought process I also thought about higher forces openly stating 'ain't spoke to god in a while I wonder what he would say?' I'm not an overly religious guy, I prefer to see myself as more of a spiritual person but I do believe in god and especially as a child I read bible stories that I found to be good lessons in life. I can remember being really young praying to god asking him to bless me with a life like I have now. How could I throw it all away when I had been blessed with everything I had ever wished for? This stage of my life was a testing time but life is always going to test you. It's how you deal with the tough times that define you as a man or strong woman.

It's weird how music can change the way I feel about things. I started the writing of this song in a very confused and possibly negative place. By the third verse I had found light at the end of a dark tunnel that I very much doubt I would have found so quickly without the aid of writing this song. As I started to put down the last verse everything fell into place and although I felt sorry for the things I had lost I felt thankful for the things I had. Although I 'never thought that there would be days like this' I start to focus on the importance of friendship and how lucky I am to be out on the circuit every weekend tearing up main stages at big events. I talk of my love of the studio as my sanctuary and the rave as my second home. As a rap in the track 'this was the calling I craved'. Ever since I first heard someone rap I knew it was what I wanted to do. All my life I had dreamed of people respecting me as an MC and quoting my lyrics. Now I travel to places as far as Canada and people are telling me they love my bars and I'm one of their favourite MC's. The loss of someone close to you should make you question things, but it should also make you appreciate the gift of life and all the things you have. No one is here forever. We have to make the most of the short time we have and try to listen to the right voices inside our heads as we endeavour to walk the right path.

Month Fourteen

Live N You Learn (Featuring Fatal)

'I never said I had the answers but at least man's asking the questions, and at least I admit when I'm wrong you're never too big to learn a next lesson'.

It's funny when I get to thinking about this point of the tape and the space I was in when I wrote this particular track. It was around March that year and I had just been away with my girlfriend for a break in the Cotswolds to celebrate our fifth year anniversary. We stayed in a cottage in the middle of nowhere for a few days and it was good to get away from everything and reflect on the things that are really important in life. When I was a kid I didn't see the beauty of the countryside. We would pass through remote rural areas on family holidays or trips and my mum would tell me to look out at the pretty scenery. Out of politeness I would stare out the window and ramble something about it being really nice but in reality I didn't care about nature. All I wanted to do was put my head phones back on and get back to my Dr Dre album. I preferred to visit my sister and her boyfriend in Plaistow in East London than marvel at Mother Nature. I liked the hustle and the feel of the inner city area's and would always tell my mum that's where I wanted to live. It was when I spent those days in the countryside that I realized how much I had changed and how much I did appreciate the relaxed atmosphere that goes with being somewhere like that.

If you listen to the first part of the 'Twelve Months' mixtape you get a feeling of angry emotions, edgy sounds, frustrations and angst. I think the reason the first part of the tape is like this is down to two reasons. Firstly I was listening to a lot of Trap and quite aggressive Rap music at the time so it naturally influenced a lot of the beats I was sourcing. But more importantly it really reflected how I was feeling at the time. Due to things going on in my personal life and the way I was questioning everything I wasn't in a relaxed mind state. I was on the edge, I started to look at everything from different angles and I wasn't sure on how I viewed my past, present and future. Different voices in my head were confusing me and I didn't really know where to turn, but spending that time in the Cotswolds with someone I loved and wanted to spend the rest of my life with really gave me a much needed moment of clarity. It made me remember what is important, how short this life is and how we have to make the most of the little time we've got here. We all go through emotional rollercoasters at different points in our lives where we feel uncertainty and confusion, but we have to try and get to the other side of the tunnel and out of the darkness or it will consume you and ultimately destroy you. When I returned home from the Cotswolds I felt lucky and blessed to be in my position in life and it totally shaped my beat selection and choice of concepts for the remainder of the mix tape. I was now in a place where I wanted to give thanks for my place, my good friends and the family around me. So I began to source more reflective soulful beats that would allow me to express these new found feelings.

I can remember the exact morning I started to write 'Live N You Learn'. I was in a really good mood the week after our break and I felt like I had to write bars. When I get the feeling that I have to write it's usually a good time to lock off my phone, go through beats and pick something inspirational because I know I'm in that zone. I can remember waking up with 'that feeling', running into the front room and downloading a bunch of instrumental's from 'Rees Beats'. 'Rees' is usually the producer I go to when I have deep rooted feelings I want to let go off. He produced my 'Behind Bars' for 'Link Up TV' and the second beat for my 'Fire In The Booth' on Charlie Sloth's Radio 1 Show. If you're familiar with either of those performances you know they are very passionate and highly charged emotional lyrical pieces but I don't honestly know if I would have expressed those feelings so eloquently without the musical inspiration from 'Rees'.

This time though, I felt like I had reached a new understanding of life. I had been through months of confusion, feelings of guilt, sadness and anger and deep rooted issues from my childhood that were all bought back to the surface. But here I was feeling happy again. Which after a bit of a bad spell is the best feeling in the world. I can remember hearing the first few bars of the beat that became 'Live N You Learn' and feeling uplifted by it. I was ready to move on from the anger and sadness and celebrate the things that are good in life and as usual I wanted to express it through my music. So as I started to bang away on the keys I thought about my time in the Cotswolds and how it made the things that are really important in life more transparent. I wouldn't call myself materialistic but I do like the odd designer garment and some of the finer things in life. I don't think there is anything wrong in enjoying the spoils of your hustle at times and going out for some nice food, drinking a bottle of 'Grey Goose' Vodka or buying yourself a new pair of kicks. It's only when the love of material goods, jewellery or expensive bottles outweigh the importance of love, family and caring for your fellow man that it becomes a problem. So as I was in a reflective mode I started the first verse with a question for my listeners to digest...

'What's it all about tell me, the Gucci belts, Truey Jeans or the LV?'

Now I have a couple pairs of True Religion jeans, a Gucci belt and some hats so I'm not saying it's wrong to stunt and wear designer clothes. But what I'm asking my listener and perhaps myself is how important are these kinds of items to you? If you are only striving to buy material goods to boost your social status or to make you happy I don't believe this will ever work. Imagine you start making that big money, you get the house and the expensive car in the drive and your still not feeling fulfilled? I believe this would be due to you not striving for the right things and subsequently feeling in a confused state about your current position in life. Having good friends, a loving family and a partner who you love and who you can trust are key elements in my own life that have made me happy. Without these factors I know I wouldn't be in the right place to do what I have to do in my personal life or my career and no Gucci belt or bottle of Grey Goose is going to help me. But nobody's perfect and I have made mistakes in my journey. Life really is a learning curve so as you live out your days you should try to learn from your mistakes and get a better understanding of how to live your life to the fullest achieving the most positive outcomes from situations you're in.

Someone who's positive attitude and love for life that has been inspirational to me over the years is 'Fatal'. I first met 'Fatez' as we call him these days when I was running MC workshops up at a centre up in Gillingham in Kent. 'Erb N Dub' would jump on the decks for a couple of hours letting off Drum N Bass, Grime and Rap instrumental's and kids from the local area's would pass through to expose their talents and skills on the microphone. With these kinds of weekly programmes you soon see who is just doing it for a bit of fun and the guys who are really dedicated to improving their craft. The thing I clocked straight away with Fatez was his passion and love for MCing. He didn't even live in Medway but he would get trains or get his girlfriend to drive him down to each and every workshop. Kids who lived walking distance from the centre didn't have the same commitment as him and I have to admit I admired his attitude from day one. I like to be around positive people and this guy didn't stop smiling. He was so enthusiastic about music so myself and Erbz started to invite him to other workshops we were doing. He would travel as far as London from East Malling in Kent to jump on the mic with other young MC's, learn different techniques and hopefully get some props from all those late nights he spent scribbling bars into another pad. Fatal is quite an infectious character to be around so even after the workshop programmes were finished we would stay in touch with him and give him bits of advice here and there. After a while he began recording demos at Erb N's studio and started coming to various parties that we were throwing. As we shared a deep love for the music and a similar drive to succeed myself and Fatez soon became really good friends. We would link up more regularly, sometimes just for a drink and a laugh. Other times he would come to my old flat on the high street in Gravesend and play me his new music and I would try to guide him on certain things. When I started to blow in the Drum N Bass scene in 2008 me and Fatal had become close, I saw him as the little brother I never had and really admired certain traits he had that I had seen in myself growing up. He was actually driving me to a lot of my early gigs and I can remember clear as day the exact moment I realized he had stepped up a gear with his music and of course the mentality that goes with it. We were travelling back from a show in Oxford and he played me a new freestyle he had recorded. The first thing I noticed was that his delivery had sharpened up a lot. But what I liked about this new approach more than anything was the honesty and passion in his performance. I believed every single line that he dropped on the record and he was telling his own unique story. So I said to him that morning, I would start to help him more with his music. I would attend his studio sessions and make him re-record verses if I didn't think they were tight enough. I got my manager Dave to come on board and talk to him about things like image, standing out from the crowd and social media marketing. He continued to record, drop music videos and develop his presence on line but more importantly he began to develop his own sound. So much so that when I was writing to 'Live N You Learn' I wanted some of that 'Fatal' flavour sprinkled on the record. So I hollered at him about him coming with the chorus for the song as opposed to a standard verse. These were pre I Phone days when we were still running around with Black Berry's so I sent him on a voice note on BBM of my first verse and whilst he was having a smoke break at work he wrote the hook and sent it to me and it was spot on!!! That's another thing I like about him. His reliability and professionalism. If I asked some people to write me a hook or a verse I might not expect to get it for another two weeks. Fatal knocks the ball back each and every time and never lets me down. This is an attribute very rare these days and another reason I'll always do what I can to help him in the music game.

So with my chorus intact thanks to 'Fatez' I began to refine the first verse. I looked out at the world and all the superficial bullshit a lot of people are into it and all the fakery that seems to be applauded in the modern world. I thought about how that trip to the Cotswolds had made me personally focus on my priorities in life and how much we take for granted so I mentioned it in the bar as it was very relevant to my current outlook on life. I began to draw on personal situations I had learnt through living my own life but I wanted to share these experiences with my audience in a non-judgemental way. It's never good to come with a 'holier than though' attitude and be too preachy when you're trying to get your point across. The production put me in a zone where I wanted the delivery to be calm and laid back so rather than flip a bunch of verbal gymnastics and intricate patterns I just kept the flow smooth and focused on uplifting people with the content.

As this record was all about change and learning from the past I looked at changes through my time and questioned whether these changes were for the best or not. For instance I thought about my time growing up and how much time I would spend with friends actually talking. Whether it was a phone call, popping into see someone or linking up for a drink I used to conversate a lot more. These days I find myself communicating through applications on my phone such as 'Whats App' or texting which takes less time but can lead to ambiguous reactions. This is why we add bro, mate or babes into our written texts to make them more personable and friendly or we make a point but then add 'lol' at the end to let the person we are communicating with know that everything is OK. In a face to face conversation you can gauge all of this from body language, facial expressions and the tone of a person's voice. It would be a shame to lose out on conversation by using technology to save time. Never the less it is something I myself am guilty of.

As I move into the second and third verses, I admit that I don't have all the answers but at least I'm asking the questions. And as I rap in the second bar, 'you're never too big to learn a next lesson'. I'm learning new things every day as I experience new challenges and things I have to overcome. So on verse two I let the passive aggressive individuals know I am hip to their suggestions and no matter what happens negativity energy will not rob me of my love for getting the most out of life. I also question people's perceptions of perfection. We are fed images of stick thin almost anorexic models that are far from attractive to me but many young girls see this as the picture of true beauty, so make themselves ill with worry trying to ascertain a size zero figure. I speak out to anyone who strives to be like someone else to accept who they are and be proud of themselves and want to better themselves for the right reason. For instance I go the gym, not so I can get a six pack and compete with pop pin ups but so I can keep a good level of fitness and look at my reflection and be happy with what I see staring back at me. A wise man once told me not to watch others because whilst you are watching others you are standing still. There is a lot of truth in that statement. I've watched great musicians fall to the way side because they constantly watch the progress of others and allow themselves to feel jealous of other people's achievements. I've learnt to feel inspired by the achievements of others, salute them for their success and keep myself motivated.

I can remember the night we recorded this record up at 'Urban Chain' in South London. We had a packed studio of people in the place. 'Rees' had travelled down to take in the session, 'Paris' was in the building getting ready to lay vocals for another track, my manager Dave was in good spirits and of course 'Fatal' was smiling away making everyone laugh. My mate Angelo was pouring out strong measures of Brandy and as the track came together I realized how lucky I was again. To be surrounded with all these smiling faces, making music I believe in and that I love. These moments are more important to me than approval from record labels and all the superficial materialistic shit many rappers put in their music videos. These are the moments I know I'll remember and look back on for many years to come. Realizing how blessed I am definitely started in the Cotswolds but recording this track and the vibes it created in the studio solidified those feelings. All those thoughts of confusion, sadness and anger were now lifted and I felt free to take the rest of the mix tape into a more positive direction. I was loving life again, living but more importantly learning and I wanted the remainder of the music I recorded for the tape to reflect that.

Month Fifteen

Fine Wine & Good Company

'I work so bloody hard I'm always on the grind, so I appreciate the links up and the good times'.

I had never worked with Pete Prince before. In fact we hadn't even met. I was getting close to finishing the tape but was on the lookout for specific types of beats that represented my outlook on life at the time. I was listening back to the tracks I had recorded so far and realized this tape needed balance, both production wise and lyrically. I had seen the dark, experienced confusion and now I felt like I was back in the light and ready to enjoy myself and the music I was making again. Pete popped up on Twitter at just the right time. I checked his production credits on his profile and saw that he had produced beats for 'Black The Ripper'. Now I was excited. 'Black The Ripper' is one of my favourite UK MC's. I've also admired his music and work rate but I was particularly into his last release at the time 'Married to Marijuana'. We battered that mix tape on the roads to my P.A's. It's one of those mood albums that you put on and it flows from start to finish. There are no obvious stabs at radio play or cross over attempts, it just sounds so natural, so you can imagine how hyped I was when Pete told me he had produced records on that project. I jumped on his SoundCloud and was thrilled to hear more sample based tracks full of atmosphere and sounds that captured my imagination immediately. I'm all for creating new music and original composition but I don't think you can beat the 'digging in the crates' ideology of hunting down rare and interesting breaks, chopping them up and creating something brand new. That after all is the essence of Hip Hop from its early days over in the South Bronx when DJ's would extend the 'break beat' section of a record using two turntables and a mixer. Also, when you sample you often get a feeling you cannot recreate through live instrumentation. A record like 'Can I Live' by Jay Z which samples 'The Look Of Love' by 'Isaac Hayes' for example immediately takes me back to a decade before I was born. I can feel the struggle of that period within the music, the frustrations and the angst of that generation, all through the sample that Jay chose to use.

Pete Prince is one of those producers who knows how to take a sample, flip it and take you somewhere with the soundscape he creates. I can remember going through the plethora of productions on his SoundCloud and finding it quite tough to pick out a beat for the project as everything was so dope! But of course as soon as I heard the horns on the intro of the beat that became 'Fine Wine & Good Company' I knew my search was over. I have spoken of these magic moments before and this was one of them. You don't know quite what you're looking for till you find it but when you do, it all makes sense. I can remember it being quite late when I found this particular beat. I had planned on selecting the beat then going to bed and getting up the next day and writing to it. But as soon as I played it a couple times I found myself writing bars to it. It had a jazzy laid back vibe perfect for those long summer nights. I can remember thinking that this would be the kind of beat you would play at a summer barbeque and put everyone on a good vibe. It was one of those beats that could lift your spirits straight away. To this day, I hear it and it puts me in a good mood. Music that can do this is special so I knew I couldn't just write standard bars on it. I had to think about the pictures and words that would come into my head as the instrumental played. All I could think about was memories of good times. I looked at the working title of the beat and saw that Pete had called it 'Fine Wine and Good Company'. We were on the same page. As I wrote the first bar I decided to keep the working title and base the tracks concept around a fixture in my life that has always been important to me.

Friendship.

Deleting my initial bars which I think related to Summer, I began to construct an opus to celebrating life and the joys of having a strong foundation of friends. I've been lucky in life to always have good friends around me. Even when I was going through all that drama in Aylesbury with my step mother I would go and check my mates Melton or David Paul and everything would be cool. I was always out of that house! From the moment I got in from school till the time I had to go in, I was in the streets on my bike. I guess that's why in the end she told me I wasn't allowed to see my friends anymore. She saw it was the one thing that gave me hope and some sort of enjoyment in life so she decided to hit me where it hurt the most and snatch that away from me too. This was a real breaking point for me and I caused so much madness for her at the time that my father finally let me go to live with my mum in Kent. When I moved there I can remember meeting one of my best friends to this day. I was new in the class and the teacher asked who wanted to show me around. I can remember it just like it was yesterday a tall kid called 'Martyn' raising his hand and the teacher whose names was Mrs Dines commenting that would be a good idea as he had only joined the school recently as well. I am almost ashamed to admit the reason we clicked at first was due to a mutual love for Liverpool FC. Liverpool were top boys at the time and me and Martyn were much like other young kids of our generation, supporting the most popular and successful team of the day. Obviously we saw the light in the end and it wasn't long before we both traded our Liverpool T shirts in for Arsenal and West Ham kits respectively. Even without the shared passion for the same football team though, we would link up every day and as I was an avid Hip Hop fan already I would show him Rap's I was writing and we would listen to Westwood's shows on the radio. Before I knew it he was as dedicated to the music as I was and he had bought himself some turntables and started to DJ. We were best friends all through school and still remain close to this day. He even turned his hand to production a couple of years ago and produced most of the 'Kaleidoscope' mixtape I featured on under the moniker of 'Mista Driscoll'. This particular friendship is one that has lasted and I know well be friends for a very long time but not all friendships are like this. I have other friends who I don't see as much anymore, I have others who have moved away and I don't see at all and I have some who I keep in contact with now and again through social network sites. We all have friends we lose touch with or we don't have much in common with anymore. I always think the important thing is to remember the memories of the times you did spend because for me personally those times have a lot to do with shaping the person I have become. A lot of the people I used to hit the Drum N Bass raves with have got married and become parents now. There not on the circuit anymore like I am but I can look back on those mad weekends we spent as a unit and it makes me smile. It's good that I have retained contact with most of the original group of friends that I used to hang out with when I first moved to my mums because these people know my journey, my dreams, my aspirations and my struggles to get to where I am now. I can remember hanging out at house parties in Gravesend and spitting bars over Drum N Bass beats weekend after weekend. Some of the people who used to hit the parties still go to the odd rave or festival and they always big me up for never giving up on music when the times were hard. With all these memories of different friendships, old and new I thought about my current friendship group. I'm talking about the people who hit the raves with me now. The guys I know who have my back and always have time for me. The people I joke with in the clubs and who religiously support my music and take time to throw get-together's for my birthdays. And of course my boys who put in that graft for me, driving a ridiculous amount of miles, gassed off Red Bull and good music so I can hit up two to three raves in one night.

As the beat played I thought about two particular friends at first who have been great at organizing link ups and maintaining communication amongst my group of mates. Whenever it is one of our people's birthday's 'Kieran' and 'Scotty' always go out of their way to ring round and make sure we mark the occasion. The whole title 'Fine Wine and Good Company' really mirrors the memories I have with my friends and the times spent at various raves, concerts, house parties and restaurants. But it particularly makes me reminisce about the many times we have hit up the Preto Brazilian Steak House in Victoria South London. We have been to this spot so many times my boys call it 'our' Brazilian Restaurant. Apart from the food which is incredible, we just feel comfortable there. It's like a home from home and we have spent many a night or afternoon there, creating memories to look back on in the future. I used this spot and other places for the inspiration for my verses on the track and as soon as I did this the words began to flow at a rapid pace. As I rap on the song 'I check my balance I could have some more in my account but friends are more important and I got that there in large amounts'. The memories I have with my friends makes me smile more than any pay check I have received and I decided to pay homage to that on this track.

One thing my friends and particularly 'Scotty' and 'Kieran' are big on is communication. I have to admit I sometimes miss their calls where I'm working so hard on this music grind. I could be in the booth or have my head deep in a new flow, the phone will ring and I won't even look at it. I get so deep in what I'm doing when it comes to music that I can sit there for hours on end in my own zone and block out the rest of the world. But it isn't that I'm being disrespectful and parring calls on purpose. I'm just so engulfed in what I'm doing that if I interrupt the creative process I might not be able to get back into the vibe I was in. It may take me a few hours on even a couple days at time to get back to my people but I always do in the end. And the strength of a good group of friends is that they know this. This is why I rapped 'spitting bars in the booth, text say I'll call you tomorrow and they text back saying Don't Flop like I was Lunar or Horror'. My mates know exactly what I'm like. Even with all the good intentions in the world, I'll come out of that booth, get deep into the mix down of the song with the engineer and forget to shout them back. Even when I get in, I'll have some food, catch up with something on the TV and it ends up being too late to make that call back. The beauty of having friends who know you inside out though is that they know your real character, so as I rap at the end of the first verse 'they know I'll forget my team know me too well, these brudda's know me better than I know myself'.

As were keeping it one hundred in this book I'll let you in on a secret. I don't enjoy writing hooks as much as verses. I sometimes write two or three hooks and pick the best one after some deliberation. And sometimes it will take me a long time to get something that I consider a good chorus. In this case though, the hook came easy.

> 'Fine wine and good company, salute my brudda's for everything that they done for me,
> They want the best for me I want the best for them,
> So let me make a toast, loyal brudda's till the end,
> Its good company and fine wine,
> They got my back they wanna see me in the prime time,
> They wanna see me shine; I wanna see them shine,
> Certified family done know the co-sign!!!'

The one thing I will say about the team I roll with now is that I never feel any jealousy from any of the individuals in the circle. I always feel like they have my back and want to see me achieve my full potential. In fact, it sometimes makes me laugh that they get more offended when things don't work out for me in the music game than I do. If they feel like someone is taking the piss or I should be getting more respect or props they get angry about it and I love them for that. They actually take it personal whereas I'm cool because I'm a student of the music business and I know how the game goes. To have friends who really have your back like that is priceless and I feel lucky to have that kind of support. I talk about this a little more in the second verse and use a phrase coined by my good friend Dreps, 'Men of Morals'. I honestly believe the moral fabric in the UK has been torn over the years and this is why a lot of people get into such a mess. If you have no morals you begin to act in a way that ultimately leads to the destruction of your surroundings, your community and society in general. On a smaller scale of a friendship group the reason people seem to fall out is a lack of respect for each other. They break the moral code of what friendship is supposed to mean by betraying the trust of their mates, spreading rumours or lies fuelled by their own insecurity or jealousy. They couldn't happen in a group like mine where the moral fibre is so strong among the people within the unit. If a true friend of mine came to me talking a whole bunch of grease about someone else in the group I would question his reasons for doing this rather than going to talk to the individual and sorting the problem out in an honest way. We all make mistakes and say or do the wrong thing at times. A good friend will take ownership for his or her actions though and a forgiving friend will normally accept an apology as long as its sincere. Having that respect for each other in a friendship group is crucial. I've heard it said that 'people often act different towards you around certain people because they talk different about you to certain people'. This is definitely true of many individuals which is why I believe you have to keep your circle tight. Snakes will always try and infiltrate a strong team and corrupt the good within it but as I'm someone who tries to keep a pure heart with good intentions I like to surround myself with people with a similar outlook on life.

So to sum up the ethos of this song and my outlook on the importance of good friendship I'll break it down like this. Whilst others yearn for glitz and glamour I can honestly say I'm more happy at the Brazilian restaurant with my peoples, cracking jokes and catching up over some good food and bottles of Rose. The simple things in life give me a lot more pleasure than all that fake shit and the material status symbols so many people work so hard to obtain. As I rap in the song 'you can go Marbella, I'll be chilling in the basement, banging out some classic DNB reminiscing with Clayton, watching the Simpsons, Homer VS Frederick Tatum'. Chilling with an old friend, listening to some old school Drum N Bass or watching The Simpsons is much more appealing to me than being surrounded with bottles of Champagne and a crew of people who are only there for the limelight. I do not need a massive bank balance to feel happy. I still don't drive so an expensive car in the driveway means nothing to me. I have hardly any jewellery so ice; platinum and gold all have zero value to me.

I'll take fine wine and good company over all that stuff any day of the week.

Month Sixteen

My Life- Harry Shotta Featuring Paris

'Now I live a different life, candle lit dinners like Jessie Ware
your my night light when I kip at night'...

Not every MC is an open book. Some rappers choose to put
out an image of strength and are reluctant to show any type of
vulnerability as they think it confuses their audience. In terms
of recording tracks about relationships I haven't ever been shy
about expressing myself about girls over the years as I try to
use my music to express my real feelings. I have however been
mindful about the stories I read of LL Cool J when he released
a record called 'I Need Love' in the early stages of his career.
LL received a massive backlash from his fan base at the time
as they deemed the record too soft and were not comfortable
with a hardcore MC like LL needing love and almost begging
for it on the record. I went back and listened to the song and
without trying to disrespect a legend it was pretty corny. Even
the instrumental Cool J rapped on couldn't be described as
anything else but 'soft'. That's not to say that Hip Hop records
where an MC raps about his or her relationships have all been
poor attempts falling short of the target. I can remember the
first time I heard Method Man and Mary J Blige's classic duet
'All That I Need' and being blown away. It wasn't your typical
love song. It retained that gritty urban feel and as much as

Meth was bathing in the joys of his current relationship it still retained the edge of who he was as an MC.

I wasn't planning on making a record like 'My Life' on this mix tape but I'm so glad I did as taking my own relationship to the next stage was an important part of this twelve month period for me. If I didn't speak on this subject my synopsis of my year wouldn't be accurate and therefore I wouldn't fully be letting in the audience into my world. Whether or not an artist should have to share his personal life is another story. I think it's down to choice but with the way this mixtape was developing I think this song and the sentiments within it are necessary for the audience and the general credibility of the project.

It had been an emotional rollercoaster of a year full of highs and lows and getting engaged to my girlfriend of six years was a true highlight. I first thought of popping the question on Christmas day a couple of months before. I had reached a point in my life and my relationship where I knew this was the person I wanted to spend the rest of my life with. It might sound bad but I hadn't ever fully trusted any of my ex girlfriends before and I had never felt this type of connection with anyone. I struggled with the notion of just being with one person in all of my past relationships but with Faye it was different. I think I had fallen in love finally and I wasn't scared to admit to it or make it official by putting a ring on her finger. I can remember traipsing around so many shops looking for the perfect engagement ring in the late weeks of November and early December and finally finding one that I liked after much deliberation, hours of research and chatting to the women in the shops about what type I should go for. Everything was set, I had the ring, I was ready to fully commit and I was feeling good about everything. Then on December 21st I received a call to say my dad had passed away. I had just finished filming a freestyle in Kings Cross and I was on route to link DJ Phantasy to travel to a booking in Newquay when I received the message from my mum. I can remember being shell-shocked. Even though I knew he had been ill for quite some time it was still horrible news. If your familiar with my first 'Fire In The Booth' on Charlie Sloth's show you would know that my father was very ill and I was struggling with coming to terms with the situation but I hadn't actually prepared myself for the worst case scenario. I can remember speaking with my mum for about five minutes and then deciding to jump on the underground and go and meet Phants over in his beloved manor of West London. It was a very surreal situation as when I reached Phantasy as I had arranged to do a quick interview for a you tube channel so I put on my best poker face and answered the guy's questions. After that was over, I can remember being in the car with Phants making our way out of London. He was as chatty as ever and I realized I probably wasn't responding as much as I would normally. I had to tell him but I was reluctant to do so as that would make the whole situation more real. I can remember saying something like 'I'm sorry if I'm not my normal self tonight but I just found out my dad died'. Obviously he was shocked but I explained I would rather carry on and do the gig. For the majority of the journey I made it clear that I would rather speak about other things but it was obviously still on my mind. When we reached the club, the whole performance flew by. I managed to hold it and down and roll out my bars and it was only when I jumped on the first train back to mine from London Bridge that it really sunk in and I broke down.

This all happened less than a week before the day I had planned to propose my girlfriend. Should I hold it off for a bit due to the current circumstances? Was it right to propose a few days after my dad had passed away? Maybe it would be better to ask her in the New Year? I had all sorts of conflicting thoughts going on in my head but I came to the conclusion that I would go ahead with the proposal as planned on Christmas morning. She was a great source of support to me with this situation and I think it bought us even closer together.

In a very highly charged time emotionally for me, I asked the question on Christmas morning of 2012. We were round her parents' house and they had no idea what I was going to do so it was a bit of a surprise for everyone. To see her response and of course to hear her say yes was definitely one of those moments in life you wish you could freeze frame and revisit every now and again. It gave me and my family a massive lift and bought a bit of light into a period which was darkened by the death of my father.

So we were engaged, putting the odd bit of money into a savings count, researching wedding venues on line, chatting excitably about our future and the big day. Everything was going great and I was feeling very secure and positive in my relationship. If you had told me I would be looking forward to marriage when I was eighteen I would have laughed in your face but I was finally ready for full and total commitment and I was enjoying the early preparation of the wedding. I was recording the last few tracks for the mixtape when Rees sent me the beat that became 'My Life'. I loved it from the moment I heard it. I can remember playing it over and over in my flat but not writing to it straight away. I wasn't sure how to approach it to begin with. Then it struck me. This track needed a singer, but not just any singer. That's why I decided to holler at Paris.

I have known of Paris since she was twelve or thirteen years old. I was friends with her older sister Sami and she used to tell me about Paris and her vocal ability. She bought Paris round to my mate Mista Driscoll's spot and she recorded some rough vocals over his Hip Hop instrumentals. When Driscoll played the demos for me I was shocked at her range and presence but always the power and emotion she would put into a performance. For someone that young to be naturally doing what it takes some people years to learn was enough to make me want to work with her. But she was very young at the time and still at school so I wasn't too pushy with getting her in the studio. I took one of the demos and put it on a mixtape that we released but then I just carried on doing my thing. It wasn't till a good few years later after her working with various producers and singing in hotels overseas that Paris came back into the mix and back into my circle. I had gone round to check Driscoll on more of a social one really. Like I said he was my best friend since my first day of primary school and although he had got married and had kids, we would still link up, have a few beers and some food and talk about Hip Hop. On this particular Sunday that he invited me up I can remember him being excited about two things. Firstly a new Polish beer he had become fond of called Tyskie but more importantly he was amped off the fact that Paris was back in the country and they were working on music together. When he played me the demo of a track called 'Stay' I must have made him play it for me a good four or five times in a row. I was in love with that record. A lot of Hip Hop enthusiasts frown on RnB but I've always loved it. The production reminded me of the classic Soul/Hip Hop sound that Bad Boy Records laced for Faith Evans and Total in their heyday and Paris sounded dope on it! I was mesmerized by the maturity and growth in her delivery. I mean, she could sing from when she was thirteen. But this was different now. I could hear her emotion even more. I could hear the pain and her life experience through the vocal. She had been through so much in her life and you could really hear it in her tone. He then played me another song called 'I'm Flying'. She took the emotional connection to a whole other level on this one. Straight away I knew we had to collaborate on just one song but a bunch of records together.

By the time the beat for 'My Life' landed on my lap, Paris had been coming to the studio with us and working on material for a while so we had a nice comfortable working relationship. I had so much confidence in her at this stage that I decided to let her take the lead on the record. I could have easily recorded my verses and sent her a demo to bounce off but I wanted her to have the freedom to choose where the track should go. I did this for two reasons. The first was to see how she got on with the responsibility of the task. I wanted to build her confidence up and show her she could take control of collaboration and shape the direction it was going to go in. The second reason was to challenge myself. I'm usually in control when it comes to the direction of my music but I wanted to let go of that in this case and see where it took me. I hadn't approached a record with a singer in that way before. I had always come up with a concept, recorded my part and left spaces for the vocalist. This was a new and exciting way of tackling the collaboration for me so I sent her the beat and told her to do whatever she wanted with it.

Paris is one of those artists that writes fast. She hears something and if she makes an emotional connection with the song she hits you back with something straight away. I can recall her sending me a voice note of the main hook and even in that rough state it was perfect. Lyrically she had chosen to base the content around the happiness she had found with her partner. She was about to have a baby with him and they were in a great place so naturally she wanted to express those feelings on the song. I don't know if I would have took the record in that direction but I could definitely relate to the subject matter as I had just got engaged myself and I was in a similar situation to her. Plus it did suite the melody and overall feel of the production. Bouncing off the voice note on my phone, she inspired a very melodic hypnotic flow that fitted into the pocket of the beat and I started to write my verses for the song. I can remember writing the first verse super quick. Part of the reason was the flow I found. As a lover of patterns I based the majority of the first verse around the same flow I had come up with as it suited the rhythm of the track like a glove. I loved the instrumental; it was a pleasure to write to it and through hearing Paris's rough vocal I knew we were going to create something special together that people could relate to.

'Before you came into my life I won't lie I wasn't living right'. My first line says it all really. I'm a bit ashamed to say I haven't been the most faithful man over the years. And even if I was faithful I wasn't the best boyfriend at times. But I guess that's down to a lack of maturity and never being in the right relationship. When you finally meet that person where everything clicks that's the time to fix up, look sharp in the words of Dizzie and make sure you dedicate yourself to making that person happy. Love is one thing but respect is another and that's what I wanted to get across on this record. I have the utmost respect for my partner, I love her and I like her. She is my best friend as well as my future wife. That is rare to find and when or should I say if you do find it, my advice would be to recognize the importance and rarity of being so blessed to find someone you connect with in that way. I talk about this on the second verse more where I say 'there's no point looking in my past cause you changed me'. Stories my mates will tell you and certain characteristics from my past have no relevance to this relationship because the dynamics and the rules have changed. If you have no emotional connection with someone you're going to deal with them in a very different way to someone who you admire, trust fully and want to have a family with. So I would say a leopard can change its spots, it just has to be for the right person. Rushing into a more serious relationship just because you feel it's that time of life will never work. You have to do it for the right reasons. It's like when I talk about being 'a lost soul in the club with a coke and a JD' on this song. It's a dramatic way of putting it but it's a natural thing to feel incomplete until you meet that person you have a deeper and almost spiritual connection with. Most people want to have that one person that they feel they can give their all to and while you're searching for that connection you're bound to do some stupid shit that doesn't make much sense. I know I've done things in the past that I wouldn't do now but life is a learning curve. A mistake is only a lesson in how to do things for the better if you learn from it. All I know is I wouldn't want to lose the one thing apart from music and family that has given my life a deeper purpose and understanding of myself as man.

I've always said the best music comes from the heart and is based on your life experiences. This record is just that! Two people celebrating what the right relationship has bought to their journeys, naturally capturing the essence and passion of those connections in three and a half minutes. I enjoyed writing to it, recording it and I still enjoy listening to it. Without this opus to my fiancée the 'Twelve Month's mixtape would be much like my life before meeting Faye, incomplete.

Month Seventeen

Insights

'Behind Bars I'm still hiding, wanna find me I'm in the studio vibezin, wanna know how I really feel I won't tell you to your face but I tell you on a beat now you know my mind state!!!'

There is something special and quite unique about the production Rees Beats makes in terms of the emotional impact it has on me as a writer. When he sends me one of those piano laced beats that pulls on my heart strings from the intro I know it's going to be another moment in my journey where I have to let it all out on the production. Not every piece of music has this effect on me. Through reading the chapters in this book you can tell I enjoy a variation of beats, tempos and mood's. However, it seems that Rees has the ability through the language of his music to unlock feelings and thoughts that would perhaps remained chained if not for the inspiration of his music. I can recall the exact moment I heard this particular beat that ultimately turned into the track 'Insights'. I woke up in a writing mood. So after my usual routine of a nice strong cup of tea and a healthy dosage of Twitter I opened a new zip folder of beats from Rees. I think the original working title of the tune he sent was 'Love Story' which intrigued me enough to skip to that beat first. As soon as I heard the intensity and the melody of the piano at the start of the song I was hooked and felt completely inspired to go in with the bars. I had to dig deep again!

Sometimes I start with a concept in my head but other times I like to keep a blank canvas approach which gives me more freedom to lyrically take the content into any area I feel I want to. I can remember reloading the beat after a first listen and hearing my phone vibrate. I looked down at my screen to see an @ on Twitter. It said something like 'I like Harry Shotta but he should stick to Drum N Bass'. Now obviously everyone is entitled to an opinion and forums like Twitter give everyone the opportunity and the voice that they didn't have before to put their opinions across to artists like myself or anyone in the public eye. I couldn't help but be slightly annoyed at this tweet though. I had come from a Hip Hop background in the first place and a lot of my understanding of flows and lyrical content comes from my years of rapping and making tunes within the Hip Hop arena. Although I had perhaps blown up in Drum N Bass and a lot of people weren't fully aware of my heritage I still found that the comment bothered me. It just seemed a little ignorant in relation to my background in the Rap scene and the work I had put in over the other genres. So with the beat playing from the top and the tweet in front of me the opening line flowed exploded onto the page...

'Stick to DNB like you're giving out the orders, no limits Donny I'm smashing down borders'...

I have never liked control or being told what to do. I think it comes from the years I spent in Aylesbury where I felt manipulated and held back from doing certain things I wanted to do. Luckily I went to live with my mum when I was eleven and I had a happy childhood from that point onwards but those years are always with me and I still think about some of the crazy things I went through in the early part of my childhood. I guess that's why I rebel so much against any sort of restriction or if I think anyone is trying to manipulate me to do something I don't want to do. It's like a certain face pops in my head and my guard goes up. Even a comment on Twitter which was pretty harmless when I think about it now will get me angry as I relate it to that feeling I had as a child where I felt a certain individual controlled my life and how I functioned. Of course whoever wrote that comment wasn't really trying to restrict my musical output or push me into doing something I didn't want to do but what they had done unknowingly was supply me with a bit of fire and something to react to lyrically. I often do that when writing bars. I will see a negative comment on a video of mine on You Tube for instance and rather than write back on line I will answer back in a lyric. I hadn't a clue of how to open the verse on this track till that comment but after reading that I was scribbling bars like a maniac. It put the necessary fire into my belly and inspired me to deliver a very passionate performance on the track. As I continued to write I realized the song was heading in the same direction as my 'Behind Barz' performance on 'Link Up TV' which Rees had also produced. On that track I used the music to as a backdrop to run through my thoughts on a bunch of topics as diverse as the rising price of petrol, to the importance of family to my respect and admiration I have for Skibadee. I thought about the impact of that track and initially had the idea of turning this track into a 'Behind Barz' sequel but I quickly scrapped that idea as that was an exclusive for 'Link Up TV' and I wanted it to maintain a life force of its own on the channel. Mediating deeper on the concept of the track I came up with the title of 'Insights'. After all that was exactly what the music was bringing out of me, my real thoughts and inner most feelings therefore giving the listener true insights into my beliefs and views on a variety of topics.

After I had responded to my critic on Twitter I decided to get a little reflective and take a trip down memory lane. Thoughts of my school days began to flood into my head and I reminisced about my final years and specifically the period when I took my final exams. I can't think of a worst time for a young person to sit their GCSE's if I'm honest. I know some kids are very academic and really respond well to revising, memorising facts and obtaining good qualifications. I wasn't one of those kids though and I know a lot of my mates weren't either. I wasn't even a bad kid in school. I only got detention a few times and hardly ever got into fights with other kids. If I liked the teacher and they showed me respect I would work as hard as I could in those classes too. I didn't have a natural aptitude for Maths and Science but I can remember really liking my Maths teacher 'Mr Caleno' so I did my best in his class and I think my grasp of the subject improved as a result of that. However, when the time for my exams came I was definitely not in the right mind state for getting the best qualifications. My whole focus at the point in my life was girls and partying. Just like many people of that age, I was smoking weed throughout the week, drinking heavily on the weekends and seeing various different girls. My focus certainly wasn't Algebra, scientific facts or the history of World War One. That's why I believe it's the craziest time of a young person's life to sit their exams. There are so many distractions and things you would rather be doing that revising. I can remember going for a smoke before a few of my exams and turning up fully Red Eyed before I sat and ran through a bunch of questions I had no idea how to answer. In hindsight would I do it differently? Of course I would!!! But when you're that age you don't have the life experience to realize how important these decisions you make can be so you end up making the same mistakes as the previous generation. It's a vicious cycle. I know I could have done far better in my final exams had I focused on them more but as I rap in the song I was 'bunning tree's before I took my GCSE's so that's why I only got a couple of C's.' Even without studying that hard though I still did well in English. I love reading and expanding my vocabulary. My love for word play and having a vast knowledge of language is something that has helped me write so many bars over the years and has kept my content quite varied. People often ask me for advice and apart from the obvious attributes like work rate, studying the craft and trying to be original I think reading books is a really good way to expand your vocabulary so you aren't using the same words and saying things in the same way as every other MC. We all know the competition is strong and to break through as a rapper that stands out can be hard but having a good command of language will definitely help you write better material.

Reading fictional stories or even biographies can also be helpful in terms of how you arrange your bars. For instance stories often have sub plots that give a bit of spice and variation to the main story line. You can apply this when writing lyrics too. The best writers are very descriptive and can paint pictures with words. Ghost Face and Biggie Smalls are two of my favourites in this field. They could be narrating a story and then go off on a tangent about a particular character and depending on how strong your imagination is you immediately get a picture of that person in your head. I try to apply some of these tactics on this record as I skip from addressing my tweet about sticking to DNB into a story of my final years at school then onto another subject. People's attention spans seem to be getting shorter these days so flipping up the topics throughout verses but still weaving the subjects together cleverly tends to keep listeners on their toes as they don't know what's coming next.

Another idea I decided to explore in some depth on this record is the negative attitude towards the younger generation in this country. Where I run MC Workshops in schools and community centres I get to work with young people all the time so I get a natural sense of how they're feeling and their hopes and aspirations for the future. Obviously every young person is different but one resounding comment I always hear is that they are constantly stereo typed by people in their communities. Just because they choose to dress a certain way and they hang out on the streets in groups they are seen as gangs or troublemakers. I fully relate to their frustrations.

I can remember being fourteen and not having anywhere to go but the local shops or the park to go hang out. I can also remember the looks we would get from some older people in the community and the way the police would constantly try to move us on and search us for no reason. Now I'm not saying we were angels, we did drink and we did smoke. But we never did anything to deserve that feeling of resentment from local people within the area. Even now I work with young people who have been excluded from school for whatever reason and I find them a pleasure to work with. So I decided to write a few bars for all those kids I meet in the workshops that feel rejected by a society and pose the age old question of 'who's the real criminal?' I don't believe the kids hanging at the local shops in Air Max kicks and snap backs who are frowned upon are the real criminals. Yet the finger is constantly pointed at them by the same people in positions of power who are cutting down funding for youth projects and pushing up the prices of public transport. As I rap on the record 'there putting up the price's just to travel on the bus but yeah he got a nice suit so everyone's supposed to trust what they say like its gospel there robbing us blind, putting up the council tax like man is not supposed to mind'. There are some serious double standards out there that I see every day and as someone who works with these kids I hear their frustrations with their communities and society at large. Why do you think so many young people of all races and class backgrounds took to the streets in the riots of summer 2012? These kids are being silenced, stereotyped and being made to feel like they can't contribute anything worthwhile to the country they live in. They feel the system is designed to keep them in the positions they are in and no one is willing to help them. I just feel people are too quick to point the finger rather than boost these young people up and give them something to strive for and believe in. This is the reason I will always try to help as many of these kids as I can by continuing to run my MC workshop courses. I have seen the positive effects these programmes and courses can have not just on groups of young people but communities in general. A lot of people have said to me I don't need to be doing them anymore as I'm financially in a position where I'm comfortable but I don't do workshops to boost my bank balance. The feeling I get knowing I've helped someone focus on music and achieve something positive in their lives is so much more rewarding than a fat cheque. I might not be able to change the world but at least I'm doing my little bit to help.

As the drums break out at the end of the songs arrangement I do what I always do on most of my records and that is go out on a positive note. I've spoken about my gripes and some of the things I think are wrong with society in terms of education and stereotyping and I've put my points across in quite a blunt and direct way. But I always want to let my listeners know that as much as life is hard and we all go through personal struggles there is light at the end of the tunnel. As I rap on the record, 'these are just some thoughts on my mind' but I do hope that some sort of inspiration and understanding of how to reach your goals can be obtained through listening to songs like this. I know I have been motivated by the words of my favourite MC's over the years and of course music is entertainment but we do have the ears of the next generation. I think it's our duty to speak some sense and give a little bit of guidance through our bars from time to time.

There is so much injustice in this world and I will always speak out against it through my channel of music but I do believe we can overcome the hurdles and achieve great things. There are some excellent role models out there like Jamal Edwards who have shown young people in this country that the sky's the limit in terms of what you can achieve if you have enough talent, drive, focus and self-belief. One thing I have never done in life or even in my career is give up and I've had my fair share of personal issues and knockbacks. You can get knocked to the ground but if you rise to your feet with the vigour of a champion with even more passion and belief in yourself these actions will truly shape your future.

These are my insights...

Month Eighteen

Bye Bye Georgie

'Bye Bye Georgie on the real, if I don't tell you how I feel, I can't carry on, the rights and the wrongs I can't talk to you let me talk to the song, and it's a shame I had to write this when you was gone, alone with a beat and my headphones on, no one to talk to so I talk to the track, wishing I could say this and you could talk back'...

I was watching the semi-final of the FA Cup on Saturday. Everything was going great. I had a sick show in Amsterdam the night before and had arrived back in the UK just in time to grab a few Stella's and watch the match. Of course I was super hyped to watch this particular game as my team were playing and anyone who knows about football will tell you it's been a while since Arsenal have put any silverware in the cabinet at the Emirates. After giving away a penalty, but then coming back to make it one all the play had gone to extra time. Failing to score in the extra thirty minutes meant one thing. A penalty shoot-out. All of a sudden a memory of my dad and his reaction to a set of Arsenal penalties came flooding back to me. Thinking back to it now, I can picture it like it was yesterday. Dad had been jumping around the room screaming in excitement and shouting at the TV, for two hours rooting for his beloved team of Gunners. Then just as was the case in Saturday's game the fate of the result rested on a penalty shoot-out. I can't remember who Arsenal were playing or what the result meant to the club but I think it was something big. So big in fact that my dad could not even watch the penalties. He had to go and stand in the garden till the shoot-out was over. At the time I didn't understand how tense he could get over a football match but as I stood in my own front room watching our players run up to the penalty spot I had the same nervous feelings of anxiety and I understood why he couldn't watch that day.

That was a nice memory I had of my dad and it's those good memories that I wanted to talk about on the song 'Bye Bye Georgie'. Due to quite a turbulent and complicated time living with my dad and his wife in Aylesbury a lot of my memories of that time were stuck in the forefront of my head when I thought about my father. The time leading up to his passing he was very ill and I really didn't like to see him like that. I did visit and call him on the phone but it really affected me to see someone I had always seen as so strong gradually getting weaker and weaker. His third wife is a lovely lady that looked after him right till the end. I wish he would have found her after him and my mum separated but life isn't like that. However I can't help but think if he would have married her and not the second wife as I call her, my childhood would have been completely different.

It was the day of the funeral that it all hit me. It didn't really sink in before because I didn't see a lot of my dad over the years so it wasn't like I missed him at this point as I wasn't seeing him regularly. They asked me, my nephew Nathan, my step brother Simon and a few others to carry the coffin into the ceremony. Damn, that felt heavy. The mood was very sombre as to be expected but I was holding it together and hadn't shed a tear at this stage of the day. Then the moment that we placed the coffin down, something Simon said will remain with me forever. It was such a simple and natural thing to say but this was the moment where I realized I would never see my dad again. I can remember us gently placing my father down and Simon quietly saying 'Bye Bye Georgie'. The fact he called him Georgie made it ten times worse. My dad was George to me. A strong ex-boxer and football player from a tough family of four brothers and two sisters. A man who did what he had to do to survive, was very competitive and right until his illness became too much he was physically active. When he called him Georgie it bought back memories of what my Nan had called him. He was her youngest son and she loved him dearly. She seemed to fuss over him when he took me to visit her and I remember her showing me pictures of her Georgie as a boy. He looked just like me in those photos. I was a chip off the old block. When Simon said those words I was overwhelmed with sadness. I no longer pictured my dad in that tough exterior and strong posture. Nor did I picture him in his last days when he was very weak and frail. I thought of him as Georgie, that innocent boy in the photos with his whole life ahead of him. I knew then that it was happening and it was very real. My eyes flooded, I wasn't going to be able to talk to my dad again. I wasn't going to be able to see him anymore. I couldn't ring him and see how he was and joke about Arsenal. Georgie was gone forever.

Another moment at the funeral that was very poignant for me was back at the wake. Everyone deals with these days in their own way which is something I now understand and respect. I can remember going to my Nan's funeral and seeing my cousins being very loud, drinking and joking and feeling outraged that anyone could laugh and joke after burying my Nan. My uncle took me aside and explained that everyone deals with these tough moments in life in their own way and although I didn't get it at the time I would understand one day. I was a lot older at my father's funeral so I now understood the behaviour of different people a lot more. I understood the thinking of those characters on the stiff brandy's keeping themselves to themselves. I got why some people were laughing and cracking jokes. I knew why some were breaking down and others were comforting them. I saw all the reactions and I understood them all. Around half way through the wake, my father's wife Elizabeth surprised us all by saying they were going to show a slide show of photographs of my dad's life. I knew this was going to be very emotional to watch but I didn't shy away from the images being projected. I stood there with the arm around my sister and watched intently. There were the photos of my dad as boy in his boxing gloves standing proud with his older brothers. Images of him as a footballer. Pictures of him with me and my sisters, my nieces and nephews, his wife and her family, his parents and so many other smiling faces of people I didn't recognize but whose life he had touched. It was a magical moment for me as it made me remember who my dad really was. Because I was so hurt from the times I lived with my dad and his second wife I had these memories in the forefront of my mind. Watching that slide show allowed me to let go of those bad memories and focus on the happy times and all the good things about my childhood and my relationship with my dad. Just after he had passed my manager Dave told me this is what I needed to do. He reminded me of the time I graduated and how proud my dad was of me. I had forgotten that day and the smile on my dad's face as I got my degree. After watching that slide show I felt emotional but I also felt a sense of release and although it was a sad day I felt like I could let go of the bad memories and focus on the good times.

It was the night of the funeral that I wrote 'Bye Bye Georgie'. I was up well into the AM, Faye had tried to stay up as long as she possibly could with me bless her but had fallen asleep. I felt quite alone so with no one to talk to so I pulled up a Rees production, put my head phones on and the words began to flow.

'We learn something new every day and every day
we grow, I thought I knew it all until that slide show,
all them memories of who you really was, couldn't

remember that and that was all because, I thought about Aylesbury and all the bad times and when I thought about it only saw the sad times, but I forgot about the fun that we once had, and when I think about it, it wasn't all bad'...

My head had been clouded with all the madness from those years living in Aylesbury that I had almost blocked out all the good times. Here I was on the day of my father's funeral, finally remembering all the funny things he did, the jokes we had shared and the times we had gone on holiday together. It allowed me to say everything I wanted to say to him that I never got to while he was alive. I was literally writing this song directly to my father. Every word was as if I was having a conversation with him and I was finally able to reconnect with these feelings after all those years. A father son bond is very hard to break and although a certain someone did their best to break it all those years ago they hadn't succeeded. I thought back to what Simon had said at the funeral service and I knew I wanted to call the song 'Bye Bye Georgie' as it was those simple words that opened up all these new feelings. It wasn't a tribute to my dad in that sense but it was my final farewell to him where I got to tell him all the things I couldn't whilst he was still here.

On the second verse I deal with an issue that many people have when a loved one passes away. Regret. I talk about that time at when I graduated and my dad was there with the biggest smile I had seen on his face. Sometimes it's hard for a parent to grasp your hustle and achievements in this music game but actually getting a degree was something my dad could understand and be proud of. The main regret I have is that I didn't have more memories like this to look back on. It was rare myself and my dad had time when it was just us but I can remember having such a laugh with him when I would help him out in his work. We shared a similar sense of humour and we got on really well. He said to me once when we were alone that he would 'love for me and him to just go away and spend time together'. But we never did and that was a real shame. By the time he had split from his second wife I was a grown up, getting on with my own life. I was done with being hurt by the situation. I had to toughen up and move on or I would have had those demons in the back of my mind forever. I think my dad knew this and respected it. We both missed out on the best father/son years we could have had together but deep down beyond all the madness I knew he loved me so I was cool with our relationship. As I rap in the song 'we were close without even being close'.

I feel you learn from even the hardest things in life and what I have learnt through all of this is how precious those early years as a father can be. You don't have those years where a child is that innocent and constantly wants your attention for that long. As soon as your child hits secondary school that period is over. They don't want you around that much anymore. They want to be with their mates 24/7. That's why those years are so special and I salute all the fathers who are there for their children on a day to day basis giving them the best childhood they can. Eks Man is someone I really look up to in this business. Not only for his ability on the mic and how long he has maintained relevance in such a competitive and dog eat dog world but for his parenting. I can tell his favourite time is with his son, he lives and breathes for his boy and works hard to give his son everything he needs. That's the kind of father I want to be. I want to be there every second my child needs me because I know how it can make you feel to miss the love of one of your parents.

As I move into the third verse of the song/conversation I start to speak a little more general about the pain of death and what it means to most people. It's so final and what I have always hated about losing a loved one is the fact that we will never see them again. I do believe in god and I hope in my heart that heaven exists but do I believe it does? I'm not sure. I don't have that unquestionable faith that some do that allows me to say 'it's ok; I'll see them in heaven soon'. I love the notion of it and I wish I could believe in it but I can't put my hand on my heart and say that that is a belief I fully stand by. I guess that's why it's harder for me to accept death and the reason I say I'm taking steps to deal with it. I can be fine about things most days for instance. I get up, write bars, do gigs, have a laugh with my mates, go to the studio, go to the gym and go about my daily business. I'm not carrying around any baggage or deep regret. But then on father's day, I'll remember and it hurts. The feelings of loss and the resentment towards an individual for robbing me of those precious years I could have had and deserved with my dad come flooding back and I get angry. I try to throw those feelings to the side though. Nothing good comes from hate so I try to deal with the issues I have through expressing myself through music and I endeavour to appreciate how lucky I am to be doing what I'm doing and have great people around me. This is my ethos in life. No matter what's happened in my past and how it's affected me tomorrow is another day. Life is a blessing and we have to live every day like it's our last because as AZ said 'You never know when your gonna go'. I tried to express this through my bars in the last verse. This is why I said 'I'm staying smiling while these other man are moving vexed'. I can't fall into a trap of hate or revenge for injustice in my own life. I have to learn from everything that has happened to me and use it to make my own future better.

Writing this song was like drawing a line in the sand and moving on. It allowed me to conversate with my father through my lyrics and say things I never got to say face to face. It also enabled me to see the light in the dark once again, wipe away the tears and focus on tomorrow. As I rap on the record 'I ain't got nothing in my soul that's hateful, all I really wanna say is man is so grateful'. And that I am. I am grateful to my beautiful mother and my father for bringing me into this world and giving me a life that I have enjoyed to the fullest. I am grateful for every single friend I have been blessed to have by my side but I'm particularly grateful to my long-time manager Dave for always being there and sticking by me no matter what. I am blessed to have finally found my soul mate who I can't wait to marry and have an army of children with and I'm blessed to be accepted by her lovely family who I now see as my own. I am blessed in so many ways that if I was to list them all here I would be here for days. But one thing I will always thank god for giving me is the gift to express myself through music. When I was eight years old and the world seemed like it was closing in around me I always had my music. I could feel how deeply I was hurting inside but those tunes spinning round on my old Hi Fi always made me feel better when I felt like I had nothing else to live for. The last twelve months have been a testing time. I have gone through extreme highs and lows. Heartbreak and joy. But the music was always there. I could be going through hell, but I found refuge on that stage spitting my bars to the people. I found refuge in the booth recording this mixtape. And I found refuge, closure, enlightenment and things I didn't even know or realize about myself through writing this book.

Thank you for riding with me through the ups and downs...

Here's to the next twelve months and whatever it brings... .
Shotz

Lightning Source UK Ltd.
Milton Keynes UK
UKOW04f2226080714

234819UK00001B/28/P

9 781783 337996